Literature Circles
A Complete Guide
for the Middle Grades

Valerie Posey

Debora Bodenheimer

illustrated by Bev Armstrong

The Learning Works

Illustrations: Bev Armstrong
Editor: Pam VanBlaricum
Text design: Acorn Studio Books, Santa Barbara, CA
Cover illustration: Rick Grayson
Cover Designer: Barbara Peterson
Art Director: Tom Cochrane
Project Director: Linda Schwartz

"Poem" by Langston Hughes: From *The Collected Poems of Langston Hughes* by Langston Hughes, copyright © 1994 by The Estate of Langston Hughes. Used by permission of Alfred A. Knopf, a division of Random House, Inc.

"Swift Things Are Beautiful" by Elizabeth Coatsworth reprinted by permission of Paterson Marsh Ltd on behalf of the Estate of Elizabeth Coatsworth.

"Nothing Gold Can Stay" from THE POETRY OF ROBERT FROST edited by Edward Connery Lathem, copyright 1923, © 1969 by Henry Holt and Company, copyright 1951 by Robert Frost. Reprinted by permission of Henry Holt and Company, LLC.

Excerpt from THAT WAS THEN, THIS IS NOW by S.E. Hinton, copyright © 1971 by S.E. Hinton. Used by permission of Viking Penguin, A Division of Penguin Young Readers Group, A Member of Penguin Group (USA) Inc., 345 Hudson Street, New York, NY 10014. All rights reserved.

Excerpt from THE BRACELET by Yoshiko Uchida, copyright © 1976, 1993 by Yoshiko Uchida, text. Used by permission of Philomel Books, A Division of Penguin Young Readers Group, A Member of Penguin Group (USA) Inc., 345 Hudson Street, New York, NY 10014. All rights reserved.

Contents

Chapter 6: Tips and Suggestions

Reproducible Pages for the Teacher

Reproducible Handouts for Students

Foreword

Are you looking for a way to improve your reading program, to make it more exciting and meaningful for your students? Are you looking for a research-based program that can be easily differentiated to reach students at all levels? Then this is the book for you! We are experienced middle school English teachers who have found the answer to how to teach reading comprehension, cover standards for reading, and reach all students. We have seen many students who are eager and excited to read, and unfortunately, many students who fear and detest any type of reading. The method that we found to reach all of these students, that was an overwhelming success in our classrooms, was using literature circles. When we began this program, it was truly an experiment for us. Although we knew that the current educational research and literature recommended such a program, we had no idea how to go about actually creating and implementing one. Using the research and philosophy available, we brainstormed literature choices, rules, procedures, timelines, worksheets, and evaluation criteria necessary to launch our experimental literature circles program.

We implemented the literature circles program in our classrooms simultaneously, for a period of approximately seven weeks. Our students made impressive gains in their reading comprehension. They became stronger literal readers, and their symbolic understanding improved as well. Our students were excited about the program, and felt that they were in charge of their education. Our students were able to choose the literature to read, they were able to respond in their own format, and they were able to run their own discussions. The empowerment this reading program gave them was incredible. The enthusiasm they demonstrated was heart warming. Using literature circles, you can achieve the same exciting results with your students.

After completing our literature circles experiment, we decided to go back to the traditional reading approach. While the students still participated and enjoyed the literature, their enthusiasm, participation, and high level thinking decreased immensely. We realized then that literature circles needed to be the focus of our reading curriculum. We enjoyed seeing the students so enthusiastic about literature, while still covering our district learning results and frameworks, along with state and national standards. Based on our success in using literature circles, we have now made it an integral part of our reading program.

All students benefit from literature circles. Teachers benefit too. We wrote this book so that teachers could implement a literature circles program in their classroom with a minimum of research and planning. This necessary guide presents a step-by-step approach, including all of the teacher preparation, recommended reading lists for poetry, short stories, and novels, and examples of worksheets we used successfully in our classrooms. All of the information we present can and should be modified by teachers depending upon the needs of their students.

We hope that this book will encourage you to add literature circles to your reading program. The goal for any reading teacher should be to inspire a lifelong love of reading, and we are confident that this program is a great way to begin.

Introduction

The Literature Circles Program

The literature circles program is modeled after adult book clubs, in which members gather to share ideas, ask questions, clarify ambiguities, and evaluate self-selected literature. In the classroom, members of literature circles groups have meaningful, self-directed discussions that go beyond the literal interpretation and begin to focus on higher levels of thinking and comprehension, such as interaction of literary elements, theme, and making personal and literary connections. Because these conversations are completely student centered and because the students have selected the literature themselves, the motivation and enjoyment level of the students are high.

What is the Literature Circles Process?

The literature circles process begins in the classroom when teachers choose a variety of high interest poems, short stories, and novels. The teacher introduces these selections to the students, who then make their first, second, and third choices. Next, the teacher puts students into groups based on their choices, and the students read the material. As they read, students are actively involved with their text through margin notes, sticky notes, and journal responses, reflecting on topics they would like to discuss. The groups meet to have a true literary discussion, and then students write in their journals about what they have learned. After all groups have met, students make new choices and start a new round of discussions. During this process, the teacher is actively involved as a participant, facilitator, and evaluator, rather than the leader.

A Traditional Reading Classroom

Imagine a traditional reading classroom. All of the students are reading the same piece of literature, many of them for the second or third time. For some students the reading is too easy, and for others it is too difficult. When the reading is done, it is time for a discussion. The teacher directs the questioning and elicits short answer responses. Students look apathetic and slouch in their seats, avoiding eye contact with the teacher and their peers. The few students who respond direct their brief answers to the teacher, looking for approval that their responses are correct. Discussions are constricted by time, and as soon as students become restless or bored, the teacher moves on.

Rarely do these typical classroom discussions move beyond a literal, superficial understanding of the material. And rarely do these discussions stimulate students' interest in reading. In fact, for many, discussions such as these "turn off" students to reading, sometimes for life. When viewing a classroom discussion such as the one described above, the lack of enthusiasm, energy, and participation from most students is painfully evident. Often, even the teacher has a bored expression. After all, the discussions are the same, period after period, year after year.

The New and Improved Reading Classroom

Wouldn't it be better to see all students engaged in meaningful discussions about literature, enthusiastically sharing their thoughts and ideas in a high-energy setting? Imagine now a classroom in which students are excited about reading. They eagerly take out the literature that they have selected, and join in small groups for a self-guided, true discussion of what they feel is important in their literature. Their expressions are animated. During their discussion they refer to notes and passages of the text in order to justify their ideas. They take risks and revise their ideas and interpretations, without fear of embarrassment. Maintaining eye contact, they respond to each other's thoughts and challenge each other's assertions. "If classroom discussion is limited to the literal content of text, it is likely that students' comprehension will also be limited to the literal level. But if classroom discussion encourages elaboration, students will be given the opportunity to develop higher-level responses to text" (Alverman and Hayes, 1989, p. 308).

The New Role for the Teacher

Using literature circles, the teacher is a guide, not the leader, and can spend time observing groups, making contributions, and moving conversations to higher levels of thought. Often these discussions last the entire period, as the students have so many ideas to share.

Benefits of the Literature Circles Program

What are some of the benefits teachers and students will derive from this program?

1. Active involvement

Both teachers and students benefit from the active involvement inherent in literature circles. The most salient benefit is that all students are actively involved in every aspect of the program. In whole class discussions, only a small fraction of the students participate because of myriad factors. Changing to a small group format alleviates shyness, peer pressure, and the fear of being wrong in front of a whole class.

> [S]peaking to peers in small groups is considerably easier for students than speaking to an entire class and the teacher. Fears abound. The fear of appearing dumb, wrong, or insensitive, or of being misunderstood, misconstrued as a show-off; or the fear of offending others by offering "negative" feedback or voicing alternative opinions. For middle-school children, especially, the risks are great— for their self-esteem hinges on their acceptance by peers, to be different is to be an outcast (Tsujimoto, 1993, p. 34).

In small group discussions, there is no place to hide; all students must be involved so that the group can benefit from multiple interpretations. It is amazing which students end up leading the small group discussions, because they are often the quiet ones during whole class lessons. The students learn from each other, and not just from the teacher. This interaction provides a much deeper analysis of literature than individual study does, and students move rapidly to higher levels of understanding.

2. Meeting all ability levels (differentiated instruction)

Literature circles benefits all ability levels. The inherent structure of literature circles makes it very easy for teachers to differentiate their instruction. "Our quest in schools and classrooms everywhere is to foster success for students in their lives through becoming self-directed, productive problem solvers and thinkers... Differentiated instruction is a philosophy that enables teachers to plan strategically in order to reach the needs of the diverse learners in classrooms today... It meets learners where they are and offers challenging, appropriate options for them in order to achieve success" (Gregory and Chapman, 2002, p. x).

In their literature circles discussions students work at their own pace, stopping for clarification if necessary or reaching new levels of understanding immediately. For struggling readers, literature circles groups help to alleviate the stress of not being able to keep up with the whole class. And because students have time to reflect in their journals before discussions take place, all students, not just the "quick thinkers," have the opportunity to share their thoughts. Students who have comprehension difficulties can rely on their group members to fill in the gaps in understanding. Therefore higher level thinking is still attained once the literal understanding has taken place.

Teachers can also differentiate the literature circles groups based on ability level if they choose. Because teachers are able to observe students so closely in their groups, they may want to restructure the groups and/or choose different literature based on strengths and weaknesses of the students.

High level students also benefit from literature circles. Instead of being held back in whole class discussions, the expert reader moves beyond literal interpretations and delves into the complexities of the literature.

3. New perspectives for teachers

Teachers benefit from literature circles in many ways. It is motivating and exciting for them to see all students actively engaged in their studies. In literature circles, teachers learn with their students as they interpret literature, and may be surprised to find that the focus of their students' discussion is different from their own focus. Because students are so interested in their work, there is less apathy and fewer discipline problems. The classroom becomes a much more positive, accepting, and exciting environment in which to learn.

4. Flexible scheduling

Literature circles can fit into any schedule. Teachers may choose to spend an eight week block of time on literature circles, while other teachers may break it down and intersperse it throughout the year. The flexibility of literature circles makes them an asset to any reading program.

5. Exposure to literature and multiculturalism

During this program, students read a wide variety of poetry, short stories, and novels. This creates a classroom rich in literature, in which students share, respond, and exchange their ideas about a variety of materials. Very often students end up reading some of the literature choices and authors on their own as outside reading. Teachers tailor the literature to their students, to ensure that myriad cultures, genres, and viewpoints are represented.

6. Interdisciplinary connections

Current middle school philosophy advocates the practice of interdisciplinary teaming, and many schools have made teams a priority. Literature circles can support interdisciplinary teaching and enhance the connections that students make between subject areas. For example, the eighth grade history teacher is covering the Civil War. The English teacher may want to choose six novels or short stories that relate to the Civil War so that students are learning in tandem. The literature circles process is still being used, but the material is supporting the historical curriculum.

7. Meeting curriculum standards

Forty-six of the fifty states now have curriculum standards for core subject areas. Because standardized testing is increasingly focused on meeting the standards, teachers and administrators are being pressured to cover the standards effectively. The literature circles program is a meaningful and student-centered way in which to cover many of the reading standards. All states have different standards. Mid-continent Research for Education and Learning (McREL) has compiled standards and benchmarks from a number of key sources into one comprehensive document (see http://www.mcrel.org/standards-benchmarks/). In viewing the McREL standards and benchmarks, it is readily apparent that the literature circles program covers many of them. For example, Language Arts Standard 6 for Grades 6–8 has eleven benchmarks that can be addressed through literature circles. These benchmarks include the following:

- Understands complex elements of plot development
- Understands elements of character development
- Makes inferences and draws conclusions about story elements
- Understands the use of specific literary devices
- Understands the use of language in literary works to convey mood, images, and meaning

The National Council of Teachers of English (NCTE) also has a list of English Language Arts Standards. The following list details the NCTE standards that are taught using literature circles:

- Students read a wide range of literature from many periods in many genres to build an understanding of the many dimensions (e.g., philosophical, ethical, aesthetic) of human experience.
- Students apply a wide range of strategies to comprehend, interpret, evaluate, and appreciate texts. They draw on their prior experience, their interactions with other readers and writers, their knowledge of word meaning and of other texts, their word identification strategies, and their understanding of textual features (e.g., sound-letter correspondence, sentence structure, context, graphics).
- Students apply knowledge of language structure, language conventions (e.g., spelling and punctuation), media techniques, figurative language, and genre to create, critique, and discuss print and non-print texts.
- Students develop an understanding of and respect for diversity in language use, patterns, and dialects across cultures, ethnic groups, geographic regions, and social roles.
- Students participate as knowledgeable, reflective, creative, and critical members of a variety of literacy communities.
- Students use spoken, written, and visual language to accomplish their own purposes (e.g., for learning, enjoyment, persuasion, and the exchange of information).

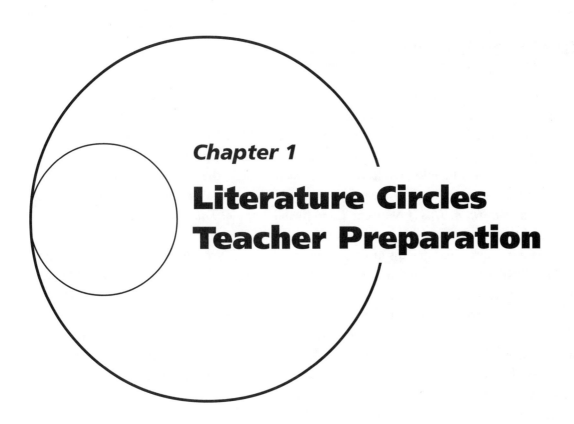

Chapter 1

Literature Circles Teacher Preparation

Introduction to the Literature Circles Program

It is 9:00 a.m. in Mrs. Ryan's seventh grade English class, and the students are excitedly taking out their books and literature circle journals. In a few minutes, they will be meeting with their groups to have the final discussion about the novels they chose to read. Mrs. Ryan overhears two students in the front row who are especially anxious to begin the group meeting. "What did you think of the ending?" one student asks. "I couldn't believe that Jonas just left," the other replies in a whisper as Mrs. Ryan reminds each group of their meeting place. "*The Giver* group, please meet by the classroom library; *That Was Then, This is Now* can go to the back table; *The Pearl* group, you may meet at the bench outside…"

The students move into their groups in various areas of the classroom and sit so they are facing each other. Yellow sticky notes containing comments and questions stick out of their books, and their literature circle journals are open to the page containing their pre-discussion response. The students are ready to begin an in-depth, student-lead discussion of literature.

What isn't seen in this picture is all the preparation that got the students to this moment in time. Before this day, the teacher chose the literature, made groups according to what each student wanted to read, modeled how to write responses to literature, and met with groups individually to teach them how to have a discussion and how to evaluate those discussions.

The literature circles process has a specific structure that stays the same regardless of the materials used. The process looks like this:

- The teacher creates a literature selection for the students, and presents it to them.

- Students choose their literature, and the teacher puts them in groups accordingly.

- Students read the literature, making notes in the margins or on sticky notes.

- Students write a pre-discussion response to the literature; they will use this during their discussion.

- Groups meet to discuss the literature, and the students evaluate each other using a teacher-created rubric.

- Students write a post-discussion response to the literature, based on new insights they gained during the discussion.

- The teacher evaluates the students based on their responses and discussions.

This chapter explains the teacher preparation needed for the implementation of literature circles. In this chapter, there are examples of handouts, literature selections, and procedures that need to be created in order to implement the program successfully. All of this information is in the same place in order to shorten preparation time. As you read this chapter, please note that all of the components will be explained in greater detail in subsequent parts; for this reason, teachers may want to read chapters 2 through 5 to get an in-depth view of the entire literature circles process, and then return to Chapter 1.

Student Handouts and Reproducible Pages for the Teacher

Throughout this book there are numerous handouts for students and reproducible pages for the teacher. These are easily distinguishable by their centered titles and the Literature Circles logo around their page numbers. Student handouts are further distinguishable by the "Name" lines in their upper right-hand corners. Complete listings of each are included at the end of the Table of Contents (page 4).

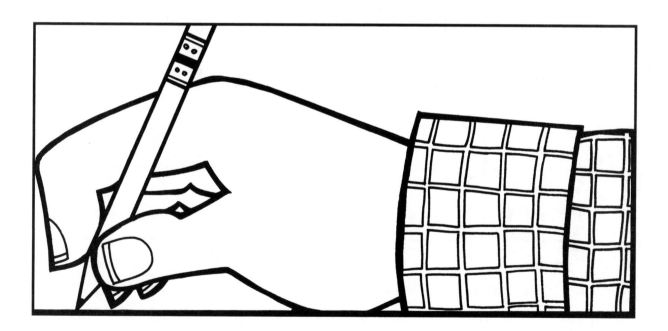

Suggested Timeline and Schedule

This is the recommended order of events for the literature circles program. Other lessons may be interspersed between segments if desired.

1. Teacher Preparation

2. Introduction of Literature Circles to Students (1–2 days)

3. Poetry—Round 1 (1 week)

4. Poetry—Round 2 (1 week)

5. Teach the high-level comprehension rubric (1–2 days)

6. Short Stories—Round 1 (1 week)

7. Short Stories—Round 2 (2–3 days)

8. Novels—Round 1 (2–4 weeks)

9. Novels—Round 2 (2–4 weeks, optional)

NOVEMBER

MONDAY	TUESDAY	WEDNESDAY	THURSDAY	FRIDAY
		1	2 INTRODUCTION OF LITERATURE CIRCLES	3
6 POETRY - ROUND 1	7	8	9	10 →
13 POETRY - ROUND 2	14	15	16	17 →
20 TEACH RUBRIC	21	22	23 THANKSGIVING VACATION	24
27 SHORT STORIES - ROUND 1	28	29	30	31 →

Selecting and Locating Materials

The first step in creating a literature circles program is to choose appropriate, challenging, high interest literature for students to read. These materials can be poems, short stories, or novels. When gathering selections, teachers should keep the following guidelines in mind:

- Students need to be able to write on their material in order to interact with it more effectively. Whenever possible, students should be given copies of the poems and short stories on which they can write.

- For novels, students should either buy their own copy in order to highlight important elements, or sticky notes can be used as markers. This will be discussed in more detail in the next chapter.

- Lists of recommended materials are provided on pages 16 through 24. In addition to these lists, classroom literature books can be used for age-appropriate selections. Literature and/or poetry anthologies are also excellent resources, as often they will group the literature by theme. One recommended example is *The Book of Virtues* by William Bennett.

- Children's magazines (with selections written by students) are also a great place to locate materials. *Stone Soup* or *Cricket* magazines are highly recommended. Students like to read material written by their peers.

- Fiction materials work better than nonfiction with students. However, depending upon the makeup of the class and the curriculum, teachers may want to experiment with some nonfiction materials. This would work well with interdisciplinary planning, or in a history/social sciences context.

Poetry

In choosing poetry, it is best to select between two and six poems (depending upon length and difficulty) that all relate to a common theme.

Themes

nature	mystery	humor
love	friendship	school
fears	war	seasons
history	courage	animals
discrimination	dreams/goals	death/loss
family	adventure	sports

The following are examples of poetry sets for teachers to use during literature circles:

Nature
"Stopping by Woods on a Snowy Evening" by Robert Frost
"Afternoon on a Hill" by Edna St. Vincent Millay
"The Pasture" by Robert Frost
"Swift Things Are Beautiful" by Elizabeth Coatsworth
"Nothing Gold Can Stay" by Robert Frost
"I Wandered Lonely as a Cloud" by William Wordsworth

Choices/Courage
"The Road Not Taken" by Robert Frost
"If" by Rudyard Kipling
"Travel" by Edna St. Vincent Millay
"The Choice" by Dorothy Parker

Animals
"The Buck in the Snow" by Edna St. Vincent Millay
"All But Blind" by Walter de la Mare
"The Bat" by Theodore Roethke
"Seal" by William Jay Smith
"Catalog" by Rosalie Moore
"Blue-Butterfly Day" by Robert Frost

Mystery

"Annabel Lee" by Edgar Allan Poe

"The House on the Hill" by Edward Arlington Robinson

"House. For Sale" by Leonard Clark

"Enter This Deserted House" by Shel Silverstein

Friendship

"Poem" by Langston Hughes (from *The Dream Keeper*)

"A Time to Talk" by Robert Frost

"Since Hanna Moved Away" by Judith Viorst

"I'm Nobody" by Emily Dickinson

"Count That Day Lost" by George Eliot

Love

"Mending" by Judith Viorst

"My Love Is Like a Red Red Rose" by Robert Burns

"no. 919" by Emily Dickinson

"Two People" by Eve Merriam

"Oh, When I Was in Love with You" by A.E. Housman

Dreams

"Dreams" by Langston Hughes

"Dream Deferred" by Langston Hughes

"As I Grew Older" by Langston Hughes

"Fifteen" by William Stafford

"To Dark Eyes Dreaming" by Zilpha Keatley Snyder

Family

"Mother to Son" by Langston Hughes

"The Courage That My Mother Had" by Edna St. Vincent Millay

"Only a Dad" by Edgar Guest

"Reading to Me" by Jeff Moss

"Lament" by Edna St. Vincent Millay

Other Groupings

Other ways to group poems might include the following:

- Author
- Poetry type (lyric poetry, sonnets, haiku, etc.)
- Literary element focus (poems with strong extended metaphors, alliteration, personification, symbolism, etc.)
- Culture
- Historical significance

Other Selections

Other selections by the previously mentioned authors are recommended. In addition, poetry by these authors is also suggested:

Angelou, Maya	Moore, Lillian
Brooks, Gwendolyn	Nash, Ogden
Farjeon, Eleanor	Plath, Sylvia
Giovanni, Nikki	Prelutsky, Jack
Herrick, Robert	Riley, James Whitcomb
Hoban, Russell	Rosetti, Christina
Hoberman, Mary Ann	Sandburg, Carl
Kuskin, Karla	Smith, William J.
Leer, Edward	Soto, Gary
Lindsay, Vachel	Williams, William Carlos
McCord, David	Yolen, Jane
McGinley, Phyllis	Zolotow, Charlotte

Short Stories

Short stories should be high interest, yet rich in theme and plot. Be sure to select stories that will appeal to all students, and that vary in difficulty and length. Themes should be universal and should cross boundaries of race and gender. Fables and myths can also be used effectively.

Recommended Short Stories

The following short stories are recommended. Teachers might want to consider other selections by these authors, or use stories that have been successful in the past.

Aiken, Joan
    "The Third Wish"

Bambara, Toni Cade
    "Geraldine Moore, the Poet"
    "Raymond's Run"

Bradbury, Ray
    "Time in Thy Flight"
    "All Summer in a Day"
    "Hail and Farewell"
    "The Drummer Boy of Shiloh"

Brooks, Gwendolyn
    "Home"

Bruchac, Joseph
    "The Son of Ktaadn"

de Maupassant, Guy
    "The Necklace"

Hemingway, Ernest
    "A Day's Wait"

O. Henry
    "The Gift of the Magi"
    "After Twenty Years"

Hughes, Langston
    "Thank You, Ma'am"

Jackson, Shirley
    "The Lottery"
    "Charles"

Jacobs, W.W.
    "The Monkey's Paw"

Jen, Gish
    "The White Umbrella"

Kipling, Rudyard
    "Rikki-tikki-tavi"

Lessing, Doris
    "Through the Tunnel"

London, Jack
    "To Build a Fire"

Neruda, Pablo
    "Childhood and Poetry"

Nihei, Judith
    "Koden"

Poe, Edgar Allen
"The Tell-Tale Heart"
"The Cask of Amontillado"
"The Fall of the House of Usher"

Rylant, Cynthia
"Papa's Parrot"

Sachs, Marilyn
"Who's on First?"

Salinas, Marta
"The Scholarship Jacket"

Sneve, Virginia Driving Hawk
"The Medicine Bag"

Soto, Gary
"Seventh Grade"

Stockton, Frank
"The Lady or the Tiger?"

Thomas, Piri
"Amigo Brothers"

Uchida, Yoshiko
"The Bracelet"

Novels

When choosing novels, look for books with strong themes, one main conflict, and non-stereotypical characters. It is best to choose a wide variety of books that are high quality, but will not need teacher direction nor excessive clarification. The Newbery Award book list is a great place to start when looking for novels. (Libraries will have updated lists.) Sequels are often a good choice. Teachers can ask their students if there are any sequels they would like to read.

Collaborate with teachers in other departments and choose books based on their units of study. This is a great way to make interdisciplinary connections. Or go online to numerous web sites to find current student favorites. Here is a list of websites that might be helpful for finding more titles:

College Bound Reading List
http://als.lib.wi.us/Collegebound.html

New York Public Library TeenLink
http://teenlink.nypl.org/

Young Adult Library Services Association
www.ala.org/yalsa/booklists

Reading Rants: Out of the Ordinary Teen Booklists
http://tln.lib.mi.us/~amutch/jen/

How to Find Books

There are many different ways to get multiple copies of books. Depending upon the size of the class, teachers need between four and eight copies of each book. Middle school teachers who have more than one English class will obviously need more books. The first place to start looking for books is at school.

- Use class sets that are not being used for whole class reading.

- The library may have extra copies of some books.

- Colleagues may have extra copies in their own classroom libraries.

- Book club bonus points can be used to obtain multiple copies of books.

- Many times parents want to make donations to classrooms. At Back-To-School Night, teachers can mention to parents that they are implementing literature circles groups in their reading program and would appreciate donations of the titles being used. Teachers can also ask parents for book donations through the school newsletter.

- School funds can often be used for book purchase. Explain the benefits of literature circles to administrators and see if they will fund the purchase of some books.

- Teachers can contact their local parent association and ask them about the availability of funds for purchasing books.

- As a last resort, teachers can hold a fundraiser with their class to earn the money to buy books, or students can be responsible for purchasing their own copies. (If this is the case, be sure to call local bookstores and find out if they have enough copies or if they can order some. Students can also order books online.)

Options for Obtaining Books Outside of School

These three options are only practical when planning well in advance.

- Public libraries are a valuable resource, and many will reserve books if you call ahead.

- Libraries frequently hold book sales at the end of the school year. Find out when these sales are because very often books are sold by the bag.

- Garage sales and used bookstores are another less expensive option.

Chapter 1: Literature Circles Teacher Preparation

Recommended Novels

The following novels are recommended. Teachers might also want to look at other selections by these authors, or use novels that have been taught successfully in the past.

Avi
  The True Confessions of Charlotte Doyle

Blume, Judy
  It's Not the End of the World
  Just As Long As We're Together
  Here's to You, Rachel Robinson
  Are You There God? It's Me, Margaret

Brashares, Ann
  The Sisterhood of the Traveling Pants

Cushman, Karen
  Catherine, Called Birdy
  The Midwife's Apprentice

Dahl, Roald
  Boy: Tales of Childhood
  Matilda
  The Witches

Danziger, Paula
  The Cat Ate My Gymsuit and sequels
  The Pistachio Prescription
  Can You Sue Your Parents for Malpractice?

Fox, Paula
  One-Eyed Cat
  The Slave Dancer

Hesse, Karen
  Out of the Dust
  Witness

Hinton, S.E.
  The Outsiders
  That Was Then, This Is Now
  Tex
  Rumble Fish

Haugaard, Erik C.
  The Samurai's Tale

Konigsberg, E.L.
  From the Mixed-Up Files of Mrs. Basil E. Frankweiler
  A Proud Taste for Scarlet and Miniver
  Jennifer, Hecate, Macbeth, William McKinley, and Me, Elizabeth

Lowry, Lois
  The Giver
  Number the Stars
  Gathering Blue

O'Dell, Scott
  The Black Pearl
  Sing Down the Moon

Paterson, Katherine
  The Sign of the Chrysanthemum
  The Great Gilly Hopkins
  Bridge to Terabithia
  Jacob Have I Loved
  Of Nightingales That Weep

Paulsen, Gary
  Hatchet
  The River
  Brian's Winter

Philbrick, Rodman
  Freak the Mighty

Raskin, Ellen
  The Westing Game
  The Mysterious Disappearance of Leon (I Mean Noel)

Sachar, Louis
  Holes

Speare, Elizabeth George
  The Witch of Blackbird Pond

Spinelli, Jerry
  Maniac Magee
  Stargirl

Steinbeck, John
  The Pearl

Taylor, Mildred
  Roll of Thunder, Hear My Cry
  The Land

Taylor, Theodore
  The Cay
  Timothy of the Cay

Voigt, Cynthia
  Homecoming and the rest of the Tillerman
  series

Zindel, Paul
  The Pigman and sequels

Recommended Nonfiction

Students found these four nonfiction authors to be very powerful:

Houston, Jeanne Wakatsuki and James D.
  Farewell to Manzanar

Jiang, Ji Li
  Red Scarf Girl

Jimenez, Francisco
  The Circuit: Stories from the Life of a Migrant Child
  Breaking Through

Rabinovici, Schoschana
  Thanks to My Mother

Journals

Creating Topics for Journal Reflection and Discussion

Once teachers have selected the reading materials for their students, they must decide how students should respond to the literature. Students must be responsible for covering certain elements of literature in their margin/sticky notes, pre- and post-responses, and discussions. It is important for the teacher to give students a structure; otherwise, they may lose their focus and become bogged down with trivialities or go off on tangents. Depending upon grade level and ability level, teachers should choose and explain items for students to investigate while they read and discuss the literature.

Literary Items for Students to Investigate

Students should

- summarize

- predict

- respond to literary devices

- discuss the theme

- evaluate

- make connections to the literature.

Some of these items should have been learned in previous years, some should be learned during the current school year, and others should be challenging to meet the needs of higher level students. Teachers should think about their priorities for student learning, including school district expectations, when deciding upon how students should respond to their literature. A natural place to start is to use the state or district standards for reading for the grade level. Teachers should include these priorities when beginning literature circles.

The charts on pages 36 and 37 are examples of possible margin/sticky notes topics, journal responses, and discussion topics for a middle school class. These lists should be posted in the classroom, and teachers should also give them to their students as handouts. It is important for students to know that they are not responsible for covering everything, but should choose relevant topics depending upon the literature they are reading. A chart of the reading standards for the grade level, based on the school district's expectations, can also be included.

Journal Responses

Students are also responsible for responding in their journals after a discussion. At this time, students should reflect on their group's discussion, and reread their pre-discussion journal response to reevaluate their original ideas and insights. See page 38 for "Ideas for Post-Discussion Journal Responses." Teachers can use this as a handout for students or make a chart for their classroom.

It is highly recommended that teachers use a rubric (or scoring guide) to evaluate student journals. Teachers should explain the rubric to their students before they begin the short story phase of literature circles. A copy of a high-level comprehension rubric is included later in this chapter with other evaluation materials, and a detailed example of how to use this rubric is included later in the book (see chapter 5). Teachers can use this rubric or create their own depending upon their needs and priorities. The rubric should cover major components of good literature examination.

Possible Rubric Criteria

Although discussion and reflection are not limited to these four areas, these criteria will help to guide the students through their exploration of the material.

- Discussing relevant literary elements and their interaction

- Interpreting the theme or themes of the literature

- Understanding multiple interpretations that exist in the literature

- Making literary and personal connections with the literature

Standards and Procedures for Literature Circles

Implementing a literature circles program requires a new approach to classroom management. While some groups are meeting, other students must be kept busy so that they do not distract from the discussions. Teachers must decide what type of classroom environment they expect during literature circles and make rules accordingly. These new rules and procedures must be modeled and taught before literature circles can begin. With rules and procedures in place, literature circles can be a wonderful learning experience. However, if rules are not established and enforced immediately and firmly, a literature circles program can fail miserably.

Grading Procedures

Literature circles programs also require a change in grading policies. Teachers must explain to their students how they will be evaluated during the program, and students need to know how to organize their materials. Students can be evaluated in the following areas:

- Journal responses

- Completion of all assignments and reading

- Participation in discussions

- Improvement and effort

- Involvement and behavior

Rules and Procedures

The following list explains categories of rules and procedures that should be considered, and gives examples for each category. Teachers can reproduce the examples in their entirety or modify them according to student ability levels and needs.

1. Rules for discussions

All students must be prepared in order to take part in literature circles. They should have the reading done by the appointed time, and they should have topics ready for discussion. It is important that every student participates during a literature circles discussion. All students should feel comfortable expressing their ideas in a supportive, encouraging environment. Therefore it is just as important that students be good listeners. Students may need to be taught speaking and listening skills. Teachers should not assume that all students know how to hold a discussion. Page 39 lists rules for discussions and rules for time not in discussions.

2. Procedures for students not involved in discussions

It is important for students to know what their responsibilities are during literature circles when they are not meeting with their group. Students must have enough work, and they must have standards set for behavior. Discussions will not work if they are continually interrupted. It is especially critical at the beginning for teachers to monitor and participate in the discussions. If teachers are interrupted and need to correct behavior, discussions will not reach their full potential. Therefore when students are not meeting with their group, they should be reading and responding to their literature. In addition, teachers should create a list of other activities for students to complete. See page 39 for ideas. Students must account for their time during literature circles, and this should be included as a part of their grade. Page 40 is an example of a student accountability sheet.

3. Consequences and rewards during literature circles time

Students must know the consequences for misbehavior during literature circles time. As with all behavior management plans, teachers must be consistent and firm. Consequences must also be ones that will not disrupt the class or the discussion groups. These consequences should fit in with the current management system, and they should be thoroughly explained before beginning literature circles. In addition, students need rewards for their good behavior. Literature circles does involve a large amount of quiet, independent work that may be difficult for some students. Teachers can remind students that their good behavior helps to increase their learning and adds to the enjoyment of the experience.

4. Journal organization

A journal is a place for students to respond privately to their literature while preparing for a discussion. They are also a place to write down reflections after a discussion. All students should know what topics they are expected to cover in their responses.

Journals should have a specific organization. This will make it easier for students to use them during discussions, and for teachers to evaluate. Depending upon the ability level of the students, teachers should assign a page limit for the pre-discussion and post-discussion responses. This limit should be clear to the students.

Teachers also must decide upon the type of journal to use. Students should not just write on binder paper and carry it in their binders. The journal responses must be bound together in some way. Some suggestions are using spiral notebooks, report covers filled with paper, small binders, or simply stapled paper packets. All journals should be the same for ease of teacher evaluation. Teachers can buy the journals and have students or the school reimburse them, or the journal can be a required supply for the beginning of the year. Keep in mind that reading and responding to the journals will be time-consuming. The journals should be lightweight and easy to carry. This will lighten the students' load as well. For examples of journal organization, see pages 41 and 42.

If teachers find that students are having a hard time organizing their journals and/or their responses are repetitive or lacking in certain areas, then they may want to structure the journals for the students at first. A sample journal packet that has been used successfully with the first round of novels is given on pages 43–53.

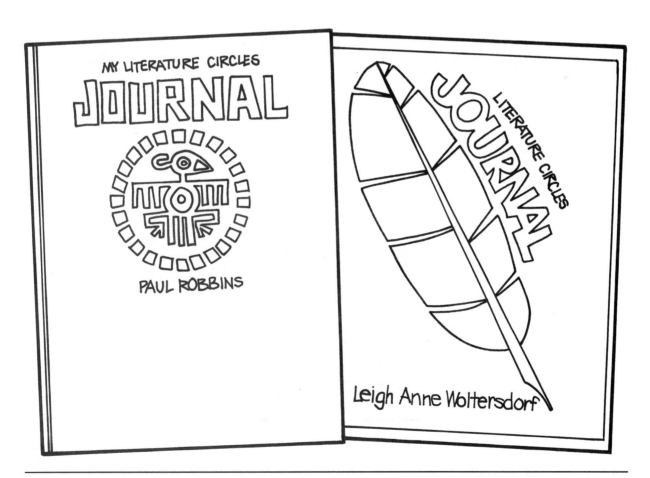

---

5. Grading policies

The literature circles process is an opportunity for all students to succeed. Literature circles stretches students to derive their own meaning from literature. Grades should be based upon effort, participation, and personal achievements.

Students should be evaluated in the following areas, and there are three handouts included for teacher use:

1. "Group Participation Record" (p. 34): This sheet can be used as a simple check sheet during each group meeting, or teachers can evaluate students with a letter grade or a plus, check, minus system.

2. "Evaluation of Discussion" (p. 35): This can be used by teachers and/or students to evaluate group discussions.

3. "High Level Comprehension Rubric for Short Story and Novel Responses" (p. 54): This rubric should be used to evaluate student journal responses. Before teachers use this rubric they should teach it to their students as explained in Chapter 5.

   Teachers should also use the "Student Accountability Sheet" on page 40 as an additional evaluation method.

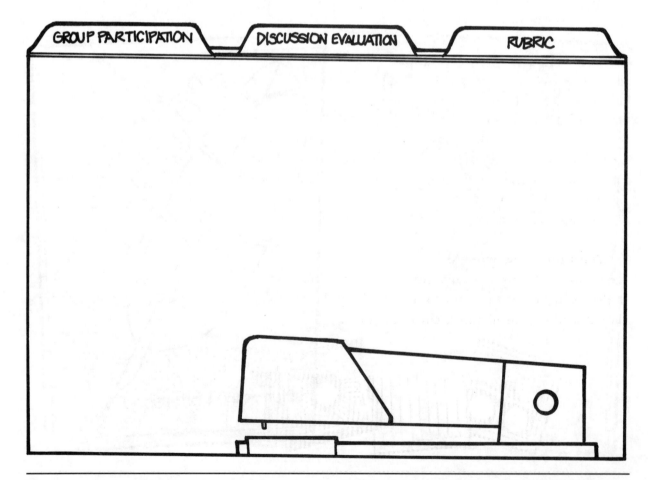

Group Meeting Times and Places

Before using literature circles, teachers must decide when and where to hold group discussions. Literature circles is a very flexible program and can be worked into any schedule. First, teachers must schedule time for students to complete their reading and prepare for discussion. For the first discussion meetings, teachers need to meet with each group individually to ensure that discussions are progressing appropriately. The length of each discussion will vary depending upon the group, but, in general, teachers should allot at least twenty minutes per group. A possible daily schedule, therefore, might have two groups meet per day, with the rest of the class time to be used for other curriculum activities. Once literature circles has been established in the classroom, and once it has been ascertained that groups are holding meaningful discussions, groups can meet simultaneously to hold their discussions. Therefore the daily schedule will change, and the program will proceed at a faster rate.

Classroom Arrangement

During literature circles, students must sit together, facing each other, while having their discussions. This can be difficult in a small classroom, especially when some students will be involved in discussion and others will be working quietly (unless simultaneous discussions are occurring). Teachers need to predetermine where literature circles discussions will be held in order to maximize the learning of all students. Discussions should not be interrupted and should be able to flow freely. However, if other students are working quietly, they should not be distracted.

The best arrangement for a classroom is to block off portions with bookshelves or partitions. These areas can be the discussion areas, with desks arranged in a group formation or pillows or small carpets placed on the floor. However, teachers should still have a good view of the rest of the classroom from the literature circles area.

Discussions can be held outside in order not to disturb other students. Outside discussions will only work if teachers can see into their classroom clearly (to watch the other students), so it depends on the layout of the classroom.

If neither of the above options is feasible, teachers can simply designate different corners of the room for discussions. Students can meet on the floor, at their desks, or around a table with chairs. During discussions other students can move their desks away from the discussion groups to ensure privacy.

See page 32 for a sample classroom set up.

Classroom Atmosphere

Literature circles posters that have been described in this chapter should be displayed prominently in the room so that students can see what they should be doing. The atmosphere of the classroom should reinforce the literature circles program.

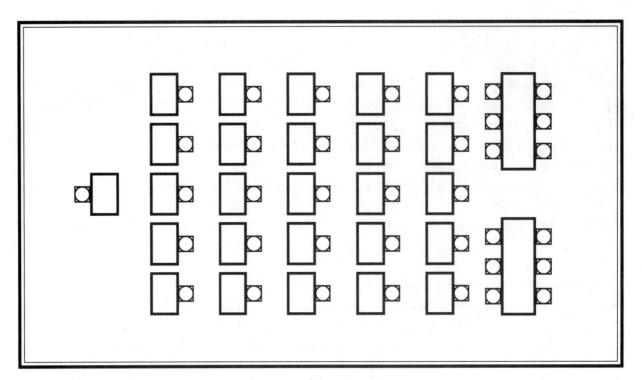

Classroom setup with the teacher meeting with one group at a back table. Other students are working at their desks or following instructions on the whiteboard or overhead projector.

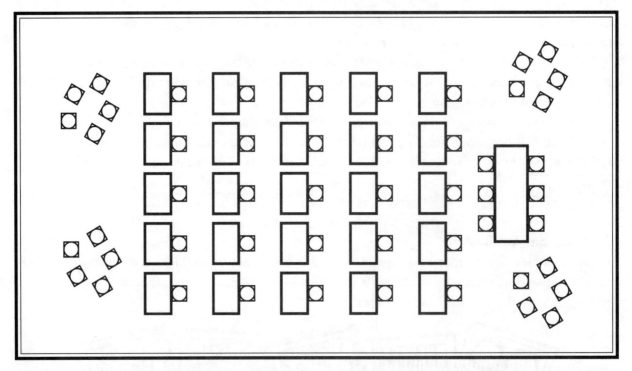

Classroom setup with groups meeting simultaneously. It is arranged to accommodate five groups: one at the back table and one in each corner of the room. Students may be sitting at desks, on pillows, on beanbag chairs, etc.

Teacher Checklist

☐ Select literature (poems, short stories, and novels).
See list of recommended titles on pages 16–24.

☐ Obtain multiple copies of the literature chosen.
See pages 21–22 for ideas on obtaining resources.

☐ Copy "Topics for Margin and Sticky Notes" on page 36.

☐ Copy "Topics for Pre-Discussion Journal Responses"
on page 37 or create your own.

☐ Copy "Ideas for Post-Discussion Journal Responses"
on page 38 or create your own.

☐ Develop rules and procedures or use pages 27–28
and page 39 for handout and chart ideas.

☐ Make copies of "Student Accountability Sheet" on page 40.

☐ Decide upon journal organization. See pages 41–53 for ideas.

☐ Decide upon evaluation criteria. See pages 34–35 and 54.

☐ Set up classroom environment and create a time schedule
for literature circles. See pages 31–32.

☐ Make copies of "Student's Literature Choice Worksheet"
on page 60 and "Making Groups Worksheet" on page 66.

Group Participation Record

Poetry_____   Short Story_____   Novel_____   Date: _____

Name	Brought Literature	Brought Journal	Journal Completed	Active Participation	Overall Impression	Comments

Evaluation of Discussion

Name: _____

Your discussion score: _____

Comments:

_____

_____

_____

_____

_____

Check Plus

- [ ] Brought text and journal to the discussion.
- [ ] Contributed often and initiated topics of discussion.
- [ ] Comments were relevant, insightful, and increased the group's understanding of the material.
- [ ] Referred to the text often during the discussion.
- [ ] Listened actively and responded to others without interrupting.

Check

- [ ] Brought text and journal to the discussion.
- [ ] Contributed occasionally.
- [ ] Comments were usually relevant and meaningful.
- [ ] Referred to the text occasionally during the discussion.
- [ ] Listened and occasionally responded to others.
- [ ] May have interrupted other students occasionally.

Check Minus

- [ ] Some materials may have been missing.
- [ ] Rarely or never contributed.
- [ ] Comments may have been off topic.
- [ ] Did not refer to text during discussion.
- [ ] Listened, but rarely responded unless asked directly.
- [ ] May not have paid attention during the discussion or often interrupted other students.

Topics for Margin and Sticky Notes

Use margin or sticky notes to create a written dialogue or conversation with the material you are reading. Through these notes you can ask questions, agree or disagree, point out figurative language, make connections, and predict what will happen next. Use these notes in formulating your pre-discussion journal response and during your group discussion.

Possible topics

1. Ask questions.

2. Summarize what you have read.

3. Clarify vocabulary (define words you don't know).

4. Make connections to the literature (either personal connections, connections to other literature, or connections to the world).

5. Note figurative language (similes, metaphors, personification, etc.).

6. Predict what will happen next.

7. Agree and/or disagree with what you are reading.

8. Point out your likes and/or dislikes.

9. Note the theme or themes.

10. React to the events and/or characters.

11. Respond to the author's use of literary elements (characters, plot, setting, etc.) and how these work together.

Topics for Pre-Discussion Journal Responses

Use specific examples and quotes to back up your ideas. Use this journal response as the basis for your discussion.

1. Summarize the literature. (This portion should be brief.)

2. Respond to the author's use of literary elements. How do these elements work together? (Examples: How does the setting affect the mood? How does the point of view affect the plot?) How do the elements add meaning, depth, and enjoyment to the poem/story/novel? Consider, but do not limit yourself to, these literary elements:
   - Character
   - Setting
   - Plot
     - Conflict
     - Rising and falling action (suspense)
     - Climax
     - Resolution/solution
   - Point of view
   - Mood and Tone

3. Examine the author's writing style. What elements exist? How do they add meaning, depth, and enjoyment to the poem/story/novel? Here are some suggestions:
   - Simile
   - Metaphor
   - Sensory Language and Sentence Variety
   - Onomatopoeia
   - Alliteration
   - Symbolism
   - Irony
   - Rhyme

4. Discuss the author's purpose/theme. Explore multiple interpretations of the theme. Is there more than one theme?

5. Make predictions and ask questions.

6. Evaluate the literature. Do you like it? Why or why not?

7. Make connections or comparisons to other literature you have read.

8. Make connections or comparisons to your own life and the world around you.

Ideas for Post-Discussion Journal Responses

1. Summarize the group's conversation with regard to topics covered. This should be brief and general.

2. Discuss the topics on which group members agreed.

3. Discuss the topics on which group members disagreed.

4. Discuss changes in your previous opinions.

5. Did your group discover new insights or ideas about the literature through the discussion? Discuss those insights.

6. Did your group enjoy the literature? Discuss why or why not.

Optional:

Did your discussion run smoothly? If not, do you have some suggestions for improvement that can be used in the next discussion?

Rules for Discussions

What to do when you're in a discussion

1. Come prepared for the discussion with your literature, journal response, questions, comments, and ideas.

2. Participate actively.

3. Listen actively and respond appropriately.

4. Stay on the subject and only discuss relevant topics. Answer questions before moving on to new topics.

What to do when you are not in a discussion

Work quietly and be involved in one of the following activities:

1. Read assigned literature, and respond to it in your journal.

2. Reflecting upon your group's discussion in your journal.

3. Writer's Workshop or other writing assignments.

4. Vocabulary.

5. Other English class assignments.

6. Silent reading and book reports.

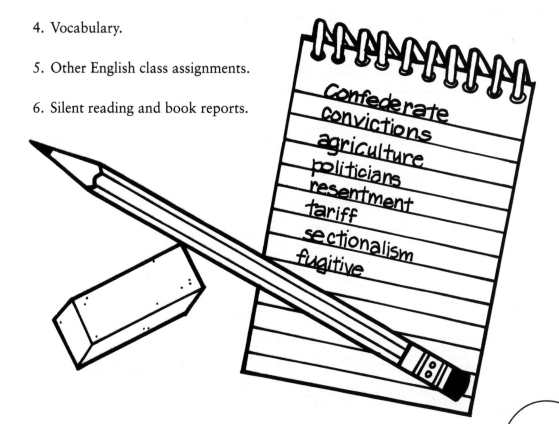

Name: _____

Student Accountability Sheet

"What I Accomplished Today During Literature Circles"

Please use the space provided to explain, in detail, all of the tasks you completed during literature circles time. For example: "I read two chapters of my book and wrote a two page response;" "I found five vocabulary words from my literature and added them to my word bank."

Monday

_____
_____
_____
_____

Tuesday

_____
_____
_____
_____

Wednesday

_____
_____
_____
_____

Thursday

_____
_____
_____
_____

Friday

_____
_____
_____
_____

Organization of Journal Entries

Guidelines for entries:

1. Do not skip lines in your entry.

2. Skip a line between entries.

3. Be sure to date and label each entry clearly (pre- or post-response and title of literature).

4. When responding to the literature, you must include a short summary. Then, be sure to consider all topics when formulating your response. *You do not have to include every topic in your response.*

5. Journals will be graded not only on content, but also on completeness and presentation.

6. You will be required to keep your journal organized, including a table of contents. Some handouts will be required as part of the journal.

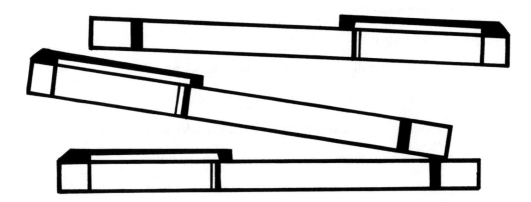

Sample Table of Contents

1. List of topics for journal responses and topics for margin and sticky notes

2. Literature Circles rules and regulations

3. Reading rubric

All of the following should be dated:

4. Poetry Set #1

5. 1 page pre-discussion response

6. 1/2 page post-discussion response

7. Poetry Set #2

8. 1 page pre-discussion response

9. 1/2 page post-discussion response

10. Short story #1

11. 2 page pre-discussion response

12. 3/4 page post-discussion response

13. Short story #2

14. 2 page pre-discussion response

15. 3/4 page post-discussion response

16. Novel: Response after discussion one (include sticky notes)

17. Novel: Response after discussion two (include sticky notes)

18. Novel: Response after discussion three (include sticky notes)

19. Novel: Response after discussion four (include sticky notes)

Note: Sticky notes are your pre-discussion responses for novels. These should be placed on binder paper with the page number next to each note after you have completed the discussion.

Alternative Journal Packet

Literature Circles Journal Packet

Title of novel: _____

Author: _____

Contents

1. Literature Circles Schedule

2. Topics for Pre-Discussion Journal Responses and Post-Discussion Journal Responses

3. Characters

4. Themes

5. Description of Setting

6. Topics for Margin and Sticky Notes

7. Pre-Discussion Response #1

8. Post-Discussion Response #1

9. Pre-Discussion Response #2

10. Post-Discussion Response #2

11. Pre-Discussion Response #3

12. Post-Discussion Response #3

13. Pre-Discussion Response #4

14. Post-Discussion Response #4

15. Sticky Notes (at completion of book)

Students: When using this packet, use extra binder paper as needed to supplement your ideas.

Name: _____

Characters

Name and describe the main characters. Use the back of your paper if you need more space.

1. _____
   _____
   _____

2. _____
   _____
   _____

3. _____
   _____
   _____

4. _____
   _____
   _____

5. _____
   _____
   _____

6. _____
   _____
   _____

Themes

Think of at least three possible themes for the book. Give evidence and specific examples to support each theme. Use the back of your paper if you need more space.

1. _____

   _____

   _____

   _____

2. _____

   _____

   _____

   _____

3. _____

   _____

   _____

   _____

Description of Setting

Describe the setting of the book. Support your description with at least one quote from the book.

_____

_____

_____

_____

_____

_____

Pre-Discussion Response #1

Be specific. Use quotes, details, and examples from the story to support your answers. Use the back of your paper if you need more space.

1. Summarize the book so far. Include the beginnings of the conflict, point of view, and mood.

   _____

   _____

   _____

   _____

   _____

   _____

2. Predict what will happen in future chapters.

   _____

   _____

   _____

   _____

3. Evaluate the book so far. What do you think of the plot? What can you say about the author's style of writing?

   _____

   _____

   _____

   _____

   _____

4. Describe the setting of the book on your setting page.
5. Add characters to your character page and describe them.

Post-Discussion Response #1

1. Summarize the group's conversation in regard to topics covered. This should be brief and general.

   _____
   _____
   _____

2. Discuss the topics on which group members agreed.

   _____
   _____
   _____

3. Discuss the topics on which group members disagreed.

   _____
   _____
   _____

4. Discuss changes in your previous opinions.

   _____
   _____
   _____

5. Did your group discover new insights or ideas about the literature through the discussion? Discuss those insights.

   _____
   _____
   _____

6. Did your group enjoy the literature? Discuss why or why not.

   _____
   _____
   _____

Pre-Discussion Response #2

Be specific. Use quotes, details, and examples from the story to support your answers.

1. Summarize the book so far. How is the plot developing? How are the literary elements working together?

_____

_____

_____

_____

_____

_____

_____

_____

_____

2. Predict what will happen in future chapters.

_____

_____

_____

_____

_____

_____

_____

_____

_____

3. Add themes to your theme page. Give details to support them.
4. Add more to your description of the setting of the book.
5. Add characters to your character page and describe them or add more to past descriptions.

Post-Discussion Response #2

1. Summarize the group's conversation in regard to topics covered. This should be brief and general.

   _____

   _____

   _____

2. Discuss the topics on which group members agreed.

   _____

   _____

   _____

3. Discuss the topics on which group members disagreed.

   _____

   _____

   _____

4. Discuss changes in your previous opinions.

   _____

   _____

   _____

5. Did your group discover new insights or ideas about the literature through the discussion? Discuss those insights.

   _____

   _____

   _____

6. Did your group enjoy the literature? Discuss why or why not.

   _____

   _____

   _____

Pre-Discussion Response #3

Be specific. Use quotes, details, and examples from the story to support your answers. Use the back of your paper if you need more space.

1. Summarize the book so far.

   _____
   _____
   _____
   _____
   _____
   _____

2. Predict how the book will end.

   _____
   _____
   _____
   _____
   _____

3. Make a connection to this book (to another piece of literature, yourself, or the world).

   _____
   _____
   _____
   _____
   _____

4. Add characters to your character page and describe them or add more to past descriptions.
5. Add themes to your theme page. Give details to support them.

Name: _____

Post-Discussion Response #3

1. Summarize the group's conversation in regard to topics covered. This should be brief and general.

_____

_____

_____

2. Discuss the topics on which group members agreed.

_____

_____

_____

3. Discuss the topics on which group members disagreed.

_____

_____

_____

4. Discuss changes in your previous opinions.

_____

_____

_____

5. Did your group discover new insights or ideas about the literature through the discussion? Discuss those insights.

_____

_____

_____

6. Did your group enjoy the literature? Discuss why or why not.

_____

_____

_____

Pre-Discussion Response #4

Be specific. Use quotes, details, and examples from the story to support your answers. Use the back of your paper if you need more space.

1. Summarize the end of the book.

_____

_____

_____

_____

_____

_____

2. Evaluate the ending of the book. Did you like it? Why or why not? Did your predictions come true?

_____

_____

_____

_____

_____

3. Evaluate the book in general. What did you think of the plot? Comment on the author's style.

_____

_____

_____

_____

_____

4. Finish your theme page.
5. Finish your description of the setting.
6. Finish your character descriptions.

Post-Discussion Response #4

1. Summarize the group's conversation in regard to topics covered. This should be brief and general.

   _____

   _____

   _____

2. Discuss the topics on which group members agreed.

   _____

   _____

   _____

3. Discuss the topics on which group members disagreed.

   _____

   _____

   _____

4. Discuss changes in your previous opinions.

   _____

   _____

   _____

5. Did your group discover new insights or ideas about the literature through the discussion? Discuss those insights.

   _____

   _____

   _____

6. Did your group enjoy the literature? Discuss why or why not.

   _____

   _____

   _____

High Level Comprehension Rubric
for Short Story and Novel Responses

Score: 5

Literary Elements: Makes insightful references to literary elements that add greatly to the understanding of the text. Makes subtle, insightful connections between different literary elements.

Theme: References to the author's purpose/theme are insightful, meaningful, and detailed.

Interpretation: Takes risks and shows originality in the interpretation. The interpretation made is not immediately obvious in the text.

Making Connections: Brings in relevant and important personal and/or literature connections that greatly add to the meaning and understanding of the text.

Draws extensively on evidence from the text to validate, expand, and reflect on ideas.

Score: 3

Literary Elements: Makes brief reference to literary elements that add somewhat to the understanding of the text. Makes obvious, predictable connections between literary elements.

Theme: References to the author's purpose/theme are superficial/obvious, not detailed, and brief.

Interpretation: Sees only predictable interpretation when readily apparent. Superficial surface understanding.

Making Connections: Will briefly mention a relevant personal or literature connection without explanation. (May let the connection dominate the response.)

Draws occasionally on evidence from the text to validate, expand, and reflect on ideas.

Score: 1

Literary Elements: Basic summary of story. (May be incomplete.)

Theme: No understanding of the author's purpose/theme shown.

Interpretation: No interpretation given. Or interpretation may be unfounded.

Making Connections: No personal or literary connections made. Or connections may be irrelevant.

Never draws on evidence from the text to validate, expand, and reflect on ideas.

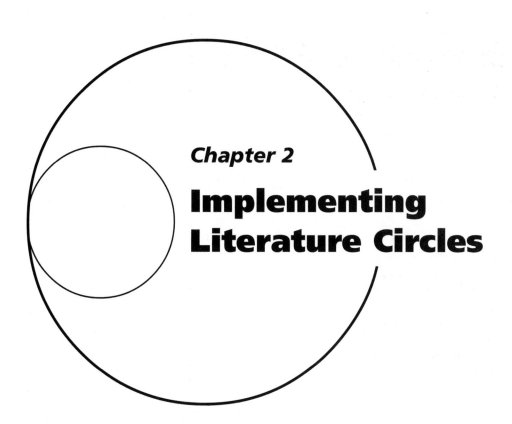

Chapter 2

Implementing
Literature Circles

Introducing Literature Circles to Students

Once teachers have completed the preparations for literature circles, it is time to begin implementation. The first step is to introduce and explain the literature circles program to students. Literature circles is a program very different from traditional models of teaching, and its success is highly dependent on the motivation of the students. Therefore teachers will need to thoroughly explain the program, be prepared to answer many questions, and most importantly, convey this information with enthusiasm and excitement.

- Students will be excited to learn that *they* are the ones who will select the literature and lead the discussions.

- They will look forward to responding in their journals when they realize that *they* choose the topics.

- They will feel empowered when they find out that their grade is determined by their participation and growth, and that they can be very successful academically as long as they put forth high effort.

All of these points must be enumerated, so that students will see the advantages of their participation and effort.

For example, the teacher might introduce literature circles with these words:

We are about to begin a new reading program called Literature Circles. In your previous English classes you probably read literature chosen by your teacher and answered questions that your teacher created. You might have had no interest in some of this literature, but you still had to read it and respond to it. Literature Circles will be different. In this program you get to choose what you want to read, and you get to choose how you want to respond and what you want to discuss. You will be meeting in small groups to discuss the literature, and therefore everyone in the classroom will get a chance to talk and share ideas. You will be learning from each other instead of just from me, and your grade will be based on your growth, effort, and participation. Therefore everyone can succeed in Literature Circles as long as you are enthusiastic and motivated.

Explaining the Literature Circles Process to Students

The following sections contain the remaining items teachers should explain to their students. During this discussion, the teacher must be prepared to answer questions, and handouts should be ready for distribution. The teacher should allow ample time for this explanation because students are guaranteed to have many questions.

Time Schedule

Begin by explaining the time schedule for the literature circles program. Whether students will be participating for two weeks or two months, they need to know the timeline and important dates and deadlines. If students are using a student handbook or organizer, this is the time for them to fill in dates, so that there are no surprises about the work expected. The teacher should explain the order in which literature circles will take place.

- The teacher should first explain that students will start with poetry, and that there will be two "rounds" of poetry. This will last for two weeks.

- Then students will read two short stories. This part of the program will last for two weeks.

- Then the class will read novels. This will take approximately three weeks, after which there will be a final project.

If possible, this time schedule should be posted somewhere in the classroom or kept in student journals, as a prominent reminder to students of their responsibilities. Teachers should also explain to students how the average day will look and how much of the day will be spent in literature circles. During the duration of the program, students should be involved with literature daily.

Literature Circles Classroom Timeline

Week 1: First poetry theme

Students make poetry selection
Read poetry, respond in journal.
Meet with group and teacher to discuss poems.
Write post-discussion response.

Week 2: Second poetry theme

Students make poetry selection.
Read poetry, respond in journal.
Meet with group and teacher to discuss poems.
Write post-discussion response.
Learn about reading rubric.

Week 3: First short story

Students make short story selection.
Read short story, respond in journal.
Meet with group and teacher to discuss short story.
Write post-discussion response.

Week 4: Second short story

Students make short story selection.
Read short story, respond in journal.
Groups meet simultaneously to discuss short stories.
Write post-discussion response.

Week 5 and on: Novel

Students make novel selection.
Read beginning of novel, respond in journal.
Groups meet simultaneously to discuss beginning of novels.
Groups decide upon time schedule for remainder of meetings.
Groups read and respond according to schedule.

March 1: first poetry theme- nature

March 8: second poetry theme- friendship

March 15: choose first short story

March 22: choose second short story

March 27: choose novel!

Choosing the Literature

The next step is to explain to students how they will choose their literature. Students will be excited to learn that they have a voice in what they will read. See page 60 for the literature choice sheet. It must be stressed here that students will not always be given their first choice, depending upon how many students sign up for a particular topic. However, students are guaranteed one of their three choices, and if there are two rounds then students should get their first choice on either the first or second round.

For instance, the teacher can say:

> The poetry themes that we will be covering are dreams, love, nature, fears and worries, mystery, and family. Some of the poems that are included in the dreams theme are two poems by Langston Hughes. These are really powerful and interesting poems that you can really relate to your own lives. The love poems are not only about romantic love, but also love that you feel for your family and friends. Some of those poems are very cute and funny. The nature poems will really make you appreciate the world around you and will definitely remind you of vacations you have taken and wilderness you have seen. [Continued explanation of all the poems and themes.]
>
> Now that I have explained all of the poems, you need to make your top three choices based on what you think you are most interested in. Please do not make your selections based upon what you think your friends will want to read. You will be analyzing these poems deeply, and it is very important that they are ones that you will enjoy. Keep in mind that you will be meeting with six different groups during literature circles, and you will probably end up with your friends at some point anyway. Choose wisely. I will tell you what poetry theme you will be reading tomorrow, and don't be disappointed if you don't get your first choice. I guarantee that during the literature circles program you will get your first choice at least twice.

Teachers can also solicit suggestions from their students regarding choices, but this should occur only after the program is fully in place. For example, if John really likes poems about sports and would like to gather sports poems, he can bring in his ideas, and the teacher can develop a theme based on those poems.

Student Discussion Evaluation

Once students understand how to choose their literature, they need to understand the discussion component of literature circles. It is now time for the teacher to explain participation grades, discussion expectations, behavior, and time management. See Chapter 1 for more details. Grade components should be posted or written out for students. After every group discussion, students will receive a written grade report from either the teacher or their peers. A suggested grade report format is given on page 35.

Student's Literature Choice Worksheet

Now that you have heard the literature options explained to you, it is time to make your first, second, and third choices.

1st choice

Title: _____

Author: _____

2nd choice

Title: _____

Author: _____

3rd choice

Title: _____

Author: _____

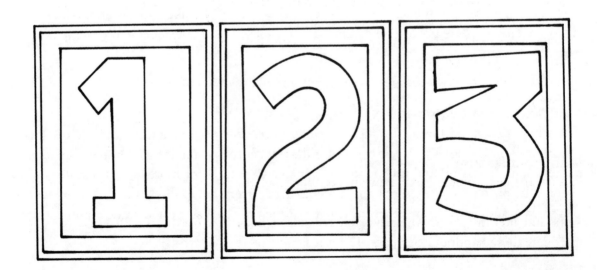

Discussion Guidelines and Examples

Rules for time spent not in discussion should then be covered. It is recommended that these rules be posted in the classroom or handed out to students. See page 39 for more details. Behavior rewards and consequences should also be discussed at this point. Here is an example of how the teacher might explain this:

> Students, today I will be meeting with the dreams and love poetry groups. Those groups need to make sure that they are ready for discussion. While I am meeting with those groups, everyone else needs to be working on one of the following options:
>
> 1. Finish reading and responding to your poetry in your journal.
>
> 2. If you are in the nature group that met yesterday, you should be finishing your post-discussion response.
>
> 3. Finish your freewrite on "If I could spend the day with anyone, it would be..."
>
> 4. You have five vocabulary words chosen from your poems due tomorrow.
>
> 5. Finish the haiku poem we started yesterday and illustrate it.
>
> 6. Read in your independent reading book.
>
> I expect the classroom to be silent as I am meeting with the poetry groups. You need to stay in your assigned seats and work quietly. If you have any questions you may whisper them to your neighbor or write them down to ask me later. Please remember that if I don't have to talk to the class or get up from the discussion group, I will add five minutes to our class party.

It is very important that the teacher has uninterrupted meetings with the discussion groups. If the teacher has to get up during a discussion to discipline students, it breaks the flow and discussion of the group and higher levels of comprehension may not be achieved. If there is a concern about discipline problems the teacher may want to involve parents in the classroom as monitors during discussion times. Parents can answer questions, ensure that all students have ample work and keep students on task. Students also need positive recognition and rewards for their good behavior during discussion times.

Journal Organization

Journals are the next topic for explanation. First the teacher must explain how to organize journals. See page 41 (Organization of Journal Entries) for an example. Students will be required to keep handouts and literature with their written responses, and therefore journals should be able to accommodate these handouts. See page 42 for a sample table of contents.

Model Journal Entries

The journal is a very important component of literature circles. Before embarking upon the program, it is highly recommended that the teacher model a complete journal entry for students. For example, the whole class can read a poem or short story together. Then, the teacher can write a response and share it with the class, have students write and share their responses, or have the class write a response collectively. The class should discuss the literature thoroughly. Teachers should then model the post-discussion response. This is also a good opportunity for teachers to reinforce the format for the journal response.

Seventh Grade Examples

The following are examples from the authors' own seventh grade classes. Before beginning literature circles, the students participated in a modeled, literature circles poetry round. The students were given a collection of love poems: "Poem" from *The Dream Keeper* by Langston Hughes; Emily Dickinson "no. 919" ("If I can stop one Heart from breaking..."); "People" by Charlotte Zolotow; "Mending" and "Since Hanna Moved Away" by Judith Viorst. The students read the poems and used highlighters and margin notes to make immediate responses to the literature using Topics for Margin and Sticky Notes (page 36). Here is an example of how one student responded to Langston Hughes by using margin notes.

I felt like this once in 6th grade when my best friend moved away.

I loved my friend.
He went away from me.
There's nothing more to say.
The poem ends,
Soft as it began—
I loved my friend.

I think the friend must have died

The speaker sounds kind of depressed here. It's like if he had to keep talking he might break down and cry.

The "soft" part and the repetition make the mood of the poem very sad to me.

Sample Student Journal Pre-Discussion Response

After taking margin notes, students then wrote one-page responses to the poems, using Topics for Pre-Discussion Journal Responses (page 37). The students were told to focus on the elements that are applicable to poetry, and if they were stuck, to begin by choosing their favorite poem and explaining why. Students wrote for approximately twenty to thirty minutes. If they finished early, they reread their responses and the poems, and added to their ideas. The students also had to create one question or interesting point to share during the discussion. The following is a sample journal response, including all of the poems:

> All of these poems have a central theme of love. The love is different according to the poem. In "Poem" by Langston Hughes it's a sad, lost love of a friend who has gone away. I think the friend died, and that is why the mood and tone of the poem are so sad. Emily Dickinson writes about the love of helping others and the love of having a complete life. Charlotte Zolotow has a contrast in her theme. It is love and sadness, or love and emptiness. Both poems by Judith Viorst are humorous love

poems. "Mending" makes light of a broken heart, with excellent metaphors. "Since Hanna Moved Away" is really sad, but cute, with good similes and hyperbole ("flowers smell like halibut"). I can really picture how it feels when a friend moves away, and it reminded me of when Josh went to private school for middle school, and I was all alone on the first day of school. I enjoy love poems, and I think out of these I enjoyed "Since Hanna Moved Away" the most because of the language and the fact that I could really relate to it.

Sample Poetry Discussion

After everyone was done writing, the students participated in a poetry discussion. The students were told that when they met in groups, the teacher would not be starting or leading the discussion. In addition, they would not have to raise their hands to participate. However, since this was a whole class conversation, every day standards were maintained, and the teacher led the discussion. The teacher started out by saying, "Who has an interesting comment or question to ask about any of the poems?" Once students began to share their ideas, they called on the next person for discussion so that the teacher would not be leading the class. For example, part of the discussion went this way:

Student 1: I liked the Langston Hughes poem because it was short and to the point. It didn't drag on and whine about losing a friend.

Student 2: Well, I didn't like the poem because I thought it was too short and I wanted to know more details. What happened to the friend?

Student 3: I thought that the friend died and that was why the speaker used such short phrases. He was too emotional to go on, like in the line, "There's nothing more to say."

Student 1: I agree that the friend died. And the repetition made the tone even more sad and final.

Student 2: But I still don't get it. I think the friend could have moved away or maybe even they got into a fight.

Teacher: Notice that all of you have different ideas and likes and dislikes. Keep in mind that poems are open to interpretation and can have many different meanings.

Student 4: When I read this poem it really reminded me of when my best friend Charlie moved to Canada when I was in fourth grade. I really felt like the speaker of this poem, because even though my friend didn't die, our friendship did.

Students continued this discussion for about twenty minutes, discussing all of the poems and their meanings.

Sample Student Journal Post-Discussion Response

The discussion was concluded by having the students write down any remaining thoughts in their post-discussion response. They used Ideas for Post-Discussion Journal Responses (Page 38) to reflect on the discussion and what they learned from it. The following is an example of a post-discussion response.

> During the class discussion, I was surprised to hear that so many people liked the poem "Mending" the best. I didn't personally think that poem was as good as some of the others, but maybe I just don't understand how painful a broken heart can be. The Langston Hughes poem really got people talking. I guess the friend didn't necessarily have to die. He could have just gone away or moved. A lot of people didn't like the fact that the poem was so short, but after listening to all of the discussion I think that the poem was more powerful because it was so short and to the point. I think Langston Hughes did that on purpose so that we would feel his sadness. These poems really were about different kinds of love, and I think in the future I would like to read more love poems to see what other kinds of love exist.

Journal responses can also be structured using the Alternative Journal Packet.

The following is another example of a pre-discussion response to "Reading Poems" that could also be used as a model for students.

> **Summary:** All three of the poems I read had the topic of reading, but they all had very different themes. The first poem was "There Is No Frigate Like a Book" which explained that reading can take anyone on a faraway journey, and it doesn't matter if one is rich or poor. The next poem was "Together" which showed the power of words, and how a mother-daughter bonding experience (while reading together) turned sour so quickly when the daughter made a thoughtless comment to her mother. The last poem was "Reading To Me", the simplest of the three poems. It talked about how comforting reading aloud can be, and how age doesn't matter, comfort does.
>
> **Themes:** These three poems had a common thread about reading, yet they had vastly different themes. "There Is No Frigate Like a Book" strongly emphasized how reading can be liberating, and how it can take people on journeys. The theme was that reading can free and liberate any soul. "Together" had a theme of regret running through it. The mother and the daughter were bonding and feeling closeness, and then the daughter ruined it with a careless comment. She regretted it deeply at the end of the poem, but there was no way to erase the mistake. "Reading To Me" had a simple theme of love and comfort, and it showed how important those feelings are throughout life. It was interesting that the common thread of reading reflected such different themes, and that showed just how powerful reading can be in people's lives.

Mood and Tone: All three of these poems had very different moods and tones. "Together" started out very loving and happy ("This has to be the best, the very best thing") but quickly deteriorated into regret and sadness, of opportunities lost ("and I wishing, oh, wishing wishing she were"). "Reading To Me" started out loving and stayed loving through the whole poem. I could feel the warmth as I was reading it ("And the sound of her voice would make me feel safe and sleepy at the same time."). "There Is No Frigate Like a Book" had a serious tone (especially because of its old-fashioned wording and difficult vocabulary), but the mood was invigorating and uplifting ("This traverse may the poorest take without oppress of toll"— showing how even the poorest person can take a journey with a book).

Favorites: My favorite poem out of the three is "There Is No Frigate Like a Book." I love Emily Dickinson poems in general, because she always has great rhyming and deep themes. This poem was very uplifting, and I could relate to it, because for me, reading definitely takes me away to the places I'm reading about. I also like the seriousness of the poem's tone, because I think reading should be taken very seriously and people should realize just how important a love of reading is.

Journal and Discussion Evaluation

The literature circles program is designed so that all students can succeed as long as they put forth effort and participation. Evaluation needs to be carefully discussed, so that all students are aware of their responsibilities. The literature circles program has two major components of evaluation: journal responses and discussion/participation. Teachers need to decide how much weight they are going to give these components, and this needs to be explained to the students. The Group Participation Record (page 34), Evaluation of Discussion (page 35), and Student Accountability Sheet (page 40) need to be explained to students at this time.

Grading journals is a difficult task. See page 54 for a rubric that teachers can use for short stories and novels. For poetry responses, the teacher can develop his/her own rubric or criteria for grading. Some elements to consider when grading include covering the suggested topics, knowledge of standards, thoroughness of responses, grammar and spelling (optional), thoughtfulness of responses, and improvement/growth from the first to the second response.

At this point, all of the components of the literature circles program have been discussed. When all questions have been answered, and teachers have ascertained that their students understand how the program works, it is time to begin implementation. The teacher should introduce the different poetry themes, and students should make their selections. Once all students have made their selections, then they must be put into groups. Page 66 details a worksheet designed specifically for making groups. The optimal group size is between four and six students. When deciding upon groups, teachers should take into consideration student behavior, personality traits, and ability levels in addition to literature choices. Heterogeneous groups work the best for literature circles. However, depending on the needs of the students, the teacher may want to create some ability groups for remediation and/or enrichment to differentiate instruction.

Making Groups—Worksheet

Title: _____

    1. _____

    2. _____

    3. _____

    4. _____

    5. _____

    6. _____

Title: _____

    1. _____

    2. _____

    3. _____

    4. _____

    5. _____

    6. _____

Title: _____

    1. _____

    2. _____

    3. _____

    4. _____

    5. _____

    6. _____

Title: _____

    1. _____

    2. _____

    3. _____

    4. _____

    5. _____

    6. _____

Title: _____

    1. _____

    2. _____

    3. _____

    4. _____

    5. _____

    6. _____

Title: _____

    1. _____

    2. _____

    3. _____

    4. _____

    5. _____

    6. _____

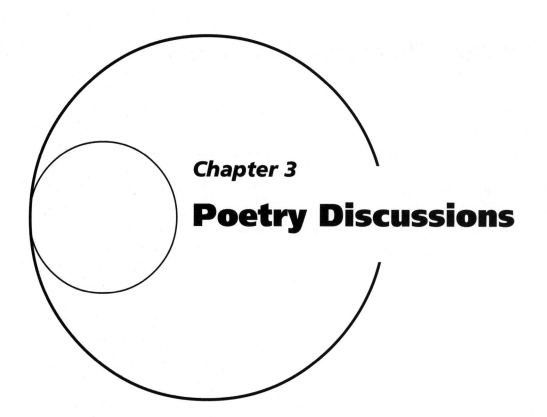

Chapter 3

Poetry Discussions

Getting Started with Poetry

There are several good reasons for beginning a literature circles program with poetry. Because poems are short and can be read quickly, students can spend more time reflecting upon and responding to the meaning of the poem. It is important that the first journal response be done during class time, so that the teacher can answer any questions the students might have about the journal reflection or preparing for the discussion. Also, although poems are often short, they are rich in meaning. A few words can hold very deep, symbolic ideas. Poems are often ambiguous or have multiple interpretations, and their complexity is a natural springboard for discussion. In addition, reading and responding to poetry is fun. Students really enjoy poetry. And because poetry is shorter than short stories or novels, it will eliminate the frustration or confusion students might feel when starting a new program.

Selecting and Introducing the Poetry

As described in detail in Chapter 2, the teacher begins the poetry component of literature circles by choosing poems that relate to a common theme such as love, friendship, dreams, adventure, etc. Poems should be chosen according to the students' reading levels and interests, and should take into account the district's curriculum and/or the state frameworks.

The teacher introduces each of the poetry themes, and students select their first, second, and third choices. Using the "Making Groups" worksheet on page 66, the teacher can then make the groups and balance them according to gender, ability levels, and student behavior. It is important that all students get their first choice some time during the course of the literature circles program, so teachers should keep track of which students did not get their first choice during each round.

Student Responsibilities

All students are responsible for reading their poetry set thoroughly. Teachers may need to point out to students that with poetry, two or more readings are often necessary. The subtleties and figurative language in many poems are often not apparent in the first reading. The initial reading and responding to the literature should be done individually, so that each student has a chance to make his/her own meaning of the material before sharing ideas with the group. Often, students will want to go immediately to their peers and begin discussing. Although this enthusiasm is wonderful and exciting for teachers to see, students do need time to ponder their own ideas first.

As students read the poems, they should jot down notes in the margin including questions, insights, interpretations, feelings, ideas about the author's use of literary devices, and even definitions of unknown words. Additionally, they should seek connections between the poems, compare and contrast them, and decide why the poems were grouped together. This is why it is so important for students to have their own copies of the poems. Examples of student comments about three different nature poems are given on pages 69 and 70.

Examples of Student Responses

"Nothing Gold Can Stay" by Robert Frost

Nature's first (green) is gold,   How can green be gold?
Her hardest <u>hue</u> to hold.   means color
Her early leaf's a flower;
But only so an hour.
Then leaf subsides to leaf.
So (Eden) sank to grief,
So dawn goes down to day.
Nothing gold can stay. —— repetition of title

The Garden of Eden from the Bible

"Swift Things Are Beautiful" by Elizabeth Coatsworth

Swift things are beautiful:
Swallows and deer,
And lightning that falls
Bright-veined and clear,
Rivers and meteors,
Wind in the wheat,
The strong-withered horse,
The runner's sure feet.

Lines 2 and 4 rhyme and so do lines 6 and 8

This poem is a list of all things— just like the definition poems we wrote in class.

And slow things are beautiful:
The closing of day,
The pause of the wave
That curves downward to spray,
The ember that crumbles,
The opening flower,
And the ox that moves on
In the quiet of power.

This really sums up the poem. All of nature is very powerful.

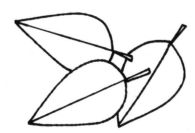

The First Journal Response

After the students read and write down initial thoughts, they will respond in detail in their journals. The first journal response is often very difficult. (Modeling a journal entry, as detailed in the previous chapter, will make this step much easier.) Students should begin their entries by briefly telling what the poem/poetry set was about, but the summary should not dominate the response. Students should use the handout entitled, "Topics for Pre-Discussion Journal Responses" (page 37) to guide their responses. The following is a sample student pre-discussion response to the two nature poems on page 69.

Sample Student Pre-Discussion Journal Response

"Nothing Gold Can Stay" by Robert Frost is about how beautiful things in nature can't last forever. "Her early leaf's a flower; but only so an hour" tells me that things have to come to an end. I think this poem may be talking about something more than just nature, but I don't really understand it completely.

"Swift Things are Beautiful" by Elizabeth Coatsworth shows that nature can be gentle (the opening flower) and destructive (lightning that falls), but that both things are beautiful. The speaker of this poem shows a love for nature just like in "Afternoon on a Hill." Because I like the outdoors, I really liked all of these poems.

Here is another example of a student's response after reading Edna St. Vincent Millay's "Afternoon on a Hill."

In the poem "Afternoon on a Hill" by Edna St. Vincent Millay, the speaker of the poem talks about how she wants to spend the day on a hill looking at flowers, cliffs, clouds, and the wind rustling the grass. You can tell she really appreciates nature and does not want to disturb it when she says, "I will touch a hundred flowers and not pick one". The mood of the poem is calm and peaceful. I can really relate to this poem, because I also have a place I like to go to be alone and enjoy nature. I go camping at the same place every summer, and there is a hike to a gorgeous, rushing waterfall. I like to go there with a book, and just sit and relax and enjoy the surroundings.

Teachers must decide for themselves whether or not to evaluate students based upon their ideas and content only, or to include organization, mechanics, and spelling in the evaluation as well. Students need to know the evaluation criteria before they write their first entry.

The students need to bring their poems and their journals with them to their first discussion.

Poetry Discussions

The First Meeting

It is now time for the first round of poetry discussions. Before the group meets, teachers should review three things:

- guidelines for students who will not be involved in the literature discussion circle

- rewards for students who participate appropriately

- consequences for negative behavior

When the group meets in its designated comfortable spot in the room, the teacher should begin by reviewing the rules for discussions with the students. It is also important at this time to define the teacher's role in the discussion. The teacher may want to say something similar to,

> When we are in a literature circle, I do not want you to think of me as the teacher with all the answers. Instead, I want you to think of me as just another participant in the discussion. As we discuss the poems you just read, I want you to direct your comments to the entire group, not just to me. Remember the importance of looking your group members in the eyes, and listening and responding to each other.

Initially, students tend to look to the teacher for validation after each comment. A good remedy for this is for teachers to keep their eyes down or to keep busy with evaluation paperwork, so the students will have no choice but to look at each other.

How to Begin the First Discussion

Beginning the actual discussion may be a bit awkward, depending on the group. The students may be nervous, not knowing what to expect for their first group meeting. A good way to get the group talking is to ask a question such as, "Well, what did you think of these poems?" or "Who has a thought to share about what you just read?" or "What did you like about these poems?" This sort of prompt is usually enough to set the group in motion. Another good way to begin is for students to take turns sharing their favorite poems and giving reasons why. This will definitely get the conversation started. It is also a good idea for students to come prepared with a question or an interesting point to discuss. In this way they will begin the discussions. By the second meeting, the students will usually not need the teacher's help to begin their literary conversation.

Sample Student Discussion

The following is an excerpt of a discussion based upon the three nature poems.

Student 1: I know that "Nothing Gold Can Stay" is about how things in nature can't last, but I think that there is something more to it that I can't figure out.

Student 2: I read a book called *The Outsiders* and this poem was in it.

Student 3: I read that too!

Student 2: And in the book this boy, Johnny, figured out that you were gold when you are a kid. But then you grow up and see all kinds of bad stuff in the world, so you can't be gold any more.

Student 3: Yeah, things that are perfect can't stay that way forever.

Student 1: I get it. We have to hold on to times that are good—like gold.

Student 2: Gold must be a symbol.

Student 4: This poem is like "Afternoon on a Hill" because when it gets dark, the speaker doesn't want her day to end, but her perfect day cannot last forever.

Students will continue the discussion until they feel they have addressed all of the points they wanted to make and answered all questions. For the first few discussions, it is important for the teacher to be a part of the group. The teacher's presence helps to reinforce positive behaviors such as turn taking, maintaining eye contact, problem solving, and staying on topic. The teacher should ensure that all members are participating and that certain members are not dominating the discussions. The teacher can make sure that the group discusses the important elements in the poems and can guide the students to deeper thinking. For example, students may be discussing their likes and dislikes, and the teacher can point out that they are all referring to the metaphors in the poems. This is known as a "literary teachable moment" in literature circles.

Another example of a literary teachable moment might go this way. A student has just noticed that in the poem "Afternoon on a Hill" there is alliteration in the second stanza. The teacher could point out that alliteration is often used to convey mood in the poem. In this instance, the words *cliffs*, *clouds*, and *quiet* add to the calm and serene mood of the speaker. The teacher can also note that alliteration is not based upon letters but initial sounds of words. After the teacher points out these things, the discussion can continue with other student responses and ideas.

Poetry discussions usually last twenty to thirty minutes. However, if students feel that they have more to discuss or would like to do some more thinking or research and then meet again, they should be allowed to do so. This second meeting may be either with or without the teacher. Teachers must remember that in literature circles, the students need to feel ownership of the literature and the discussion.

Post-Discussion for Poetry

The Post-Discussion Response

Either directly after the meeting or for homework that night, students should go back to their journals and complete a post-discussion response. It is optimal for students to write their post-responses immediately after the discussion. However, due to time constraints, some students may have to complete their responses at home. The post-response can include new insights gained during the discussion, changes in initial thoughts or interpretations of the poems, and overall impressions of the discussion. The post response should *not*, however, be a narrative account of the entire discussion. "Amy said that Frost used extended metaphor. Then Charlie said that gold symbolized something new and perfect. Shannon said that she agreed...." To avoid such responses it is highly recommended that teachers model a post-discussion response prior to embarking upon the program.

Here is an example of a post-discussion response to the three nature poems.

Sample Student Post-Discussion Journal Response

I feel like I understand these poems better now. I didn't realize that Millay used a great alliteration in her poem when she wrote, "I will look at the cliffs and clouds with quiet eyes." We talked about how authors usually have a purpose for using alliteration, and in this poem, the alliteration makes you feel very calm. I also really understand the poem "Nothing Gold" a lot better. When things are new and fresh and young, they are gold. But then gold things get spoiled. I think the theme of this poem is that we have to appreciate the "gold" in life because it will not be there forever. After we discussed this poem in detail, the whole group decided this was our favorite poem because it can mean so many things, and it really applies to all of our lives.

The Second Round of Poetry Discussions

After the teacher has met with all of the groups individually, a second round of poetry discussions is advised. In the second round, the students are more comfortable with the procedures, and therefore the discussions are livelier and more in-depth. The teacher can make the new groups based upon the initial choices the students made, or the themes can be reintroduced and students can again select their first, second, and third choices. The latter is a better option, especially if one of the poetry sets did not work well, and another theme needs to be introduced.

Students again read, make notes, write journal responses, meet for a discussion with the teacher, and reflect upon the discussion in a post-response. It is important that the teacher again meet with each group in order to guide the students and to model positive discussion procedures.

Poetry Evaluation

Teachers need to decide for themselves how much emphasis to place on the evaluation of the discussion versus the evaluation of the journals. For some students, the discussion is a better measure of achievement because their oral language is more developed than their writing. For other students, the converse is true. However, it is imperative for the success of the literature circles program that the students receive constructive feedback in both areas.

Evaluating Discussions

The easiest and most efficient way to evaluate student discussion is to jot down notes on the "Group Participation Record", page 34, during the discussions. Teachers who have laptop computers may even want to take anecdotal records during the group discussions. Some teachers find it helpful to tape record the discussions, because it is difficult to act as a group member and evaluator at the same time. Listening to all the tapes, however, can become a cumbersome and tedious task, so teachers should not depend on this as their sole method of discussion evaluation.

Regardless of the method used, students need immediate feedback about their participation in the group. A good way to do this is to use a simple plus, check, minus rubric. Teachers can give each student a slip of paper with his or her score (including comments, if possible) the day after a discussion. See "Evaluation of Discussion" on page 35.

Evaluating Journals

After both rounds of poetry are finished, journals need to be evaluated by the teacher before going on to the short story phase of literature circles. Pre-discussion and post-discussion journal entries should be checked for completeness. However, to make the evaluation a less daunting task, it may be easier to evaluate only one of the entries in depth. Each student can choose his/her best entry for the teacher to evaluate. Teachers need to take time reading each student's journal carefully and evaluate with both positive comments and suggestions. This first entry can be used as a baseline for showing later improvement. Journals should be graded, passed back, and discussed with students before beginning the short story phase of literature circles.

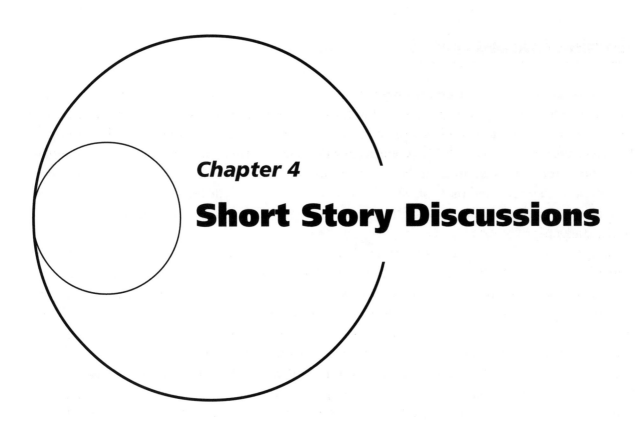

Chapter 4

Short Story Discussions

Getting Started with Short Stories

The High Level Comprehension Rubric

At this point of the literature circles program, a rubric for evaluation needs to be introduced. A high-level comprehension rubric is available for use (see page 54) and has been specifically designed for literature circles. It is highly recommended that teachers use or modify this rubric depending upon their students. This rubric has been developed to move students from literal to symbolic interpretation of literature, and therefore should be used to measure student gains rather than to simply assign a score and grade. Before using the rubric, each of the four categories must be fully explained to the students.

The teaching of the rubric should proceed in this order:

- Read a short story together as a class.

- All students write a response and then put it aside.

- Teachers put a sample response to the story on the overhead projector or pass out copies. (This response can be made up by the teacher or can be a response from a previous year.)

- Teachers guide the students in analyzing the response. The class scores each rubric area separately and discusses the scores agreed upon. (The teacher may want to mark the response on the overhead using four different colors, one for each category, so that the different rubric areas are made clear to the students.)

- Students then score their own responses using the rubric or they can exchange papers and score each other's.

Examples of Scored Responses

The following are two responses done by seventh grade students after reading the short story "The Third Wish" by Joan Aiken. Student responses have not been edited. At the end of each student's response, a score and explanation are given for each of the rubric categories.

Summary of the Story

"The Third Wish" by Joan Aiken is a fantasy about a man named Mr. Peters who frees a swan caught in a thorn bush. The swan turns into a little man dressed all in green who offers him three wishes symbolized by three dead leaves. Mr. Peters wishes for a wife as beautiful as the forest. He gets his wish, but his new wife turns out to be a swan who is transformed into human form. Because his wife misses her swan sister so terribly, Mr. Peters uses his next wish to turn her back into a swan. The two swans remain by Mr. Peters' side, keeping him company and looking after him for many years. One autumn night, Mr. Peters dies peacefully in bed with a smile. In his hands are a withered leaf and a white feather.

Response Example 1

This story was about a man who saved a swan who was stuck in thorns. For doing this, the man was given three leaves. Each represented a wish he could make. The man, Mr. Peters, knew he should be careful with his wishes; otherwise they could lead to disaster. Mr. Peters put two of the leaves away for safekeeping. He decided to use the first one to wish for a wife as beautiful as the forest. She came, but was rather unhappy. You see, Leita (the wife) was really a swan. She had been turned into human form because of Mr. Peter's wish. Leita loved Mr. Peters, but was sad without her sister who was still a swan. Eventually, Mr. Peters used his second wish to turn Leita back into a swan. She was happy then. Believe it or not, Mr. Peters stayed faithful to Leita even when she was in swan form. They were both happy. Mr. Peters died holding his last wish and a white feather, showing that he already got his third wish, a companion in his old age.

I thought the story was like a fairy tale. It had the magic of animals and people changing into each other, three wishes, and rewards for saving animals in the forest. I really like this type of writing. I especially liked how Leita loved Mr. Peters so much that she didn't jump at his offer to be turned back into a swan. And Mr. Peters loved Leita so much that he turned her back into a swan when she screamed in the night for her sister, Rhea. What was even sweeter was Mr. Peters stayed faithful to Leita all these years, even though she was a swan.

I also thought that the story had kind of a moral to be content with what you have, and to do the right thing to make someone else happy.

The main conflict of the story was that Mr. Peters had three wishes. What should he do with them? A secondary conflict was that Leita, Mr. Peter's number one wish, was unhappy as a person. I thought that the sweetness of Leita and Mr. Peters helped make the story especially nice. I really liked the ending. Even though Mr. Peters died in the end, it did not seem too sad—he had lived a fulfilling and rewarding life. He was even victorious over the King of the Forest by not using his third wish.

The climax of the story was when Mr. Peters turned Leita back into a swan. That just seemed so kind of him! The resolution was Mr. Peters growing old and still staying faithful to Leita.

As I said above, the feeling of the story was fairy-tale like. At first I thought it was going to be more of a scary story because of the empty dark road in the Savernake Forest, and the strange cries. But I was glad they turned out the way it did. I think that the theme of the story was to always do what you feel in your heart is right, the way Mr. Peters turned Leita back into a swan.

In this story the setting is the Savernake Forest, at dusk on a spring evening. Now I have no idea where the Savernake Forest is, or even if it really exists. But I don't think the story really needed to say. Like most fairy-tales, it is set in a forest. That's all the reader really needs to know about the setting.

I thought that the sentences, especially in the beginning were long and flowery. They helped create a magical mood. Perhaps I was just so engrossed in the story that I did not notice, but the sentences seemed shorter and had less fancy vocabulary towards the end.

I wonder what happened to Leita and Rhea after Mr. Peters died. Were they fraught with grief? That would be sad. Perhaps Leita and Mr. Peters died at the same time. That would eliminate their suffering.

I really liked this story. It seemed a little like Hans Christian Andersen's version of "The Little Mermaid" because in that story, the mermaid dies and becomes foam on the water, so her prince can be happy. This is similar to Mr. Peters turning Leita back into a swan so that she will be happy. I hope that when I grow up, I can be as nice a person as Mr. Peters. It seemed so very unselfish when Mr. Peters turned his wife back into a swan. I really like that story, complete with its complex sentences and vivid vocabulary. The characters, despite the magic in the story, seemed as though they could have been real. I loved the ending. I'm glad I got the chance to read this story.

Analysis of Response Example 1 (Using the Rubric)

Literary Elements: 4
- Explains characterization
- Shows understanding of the plot
- Explains story development: conflict, climax, resolution
- Describes setting
- Shows how the sentence patterns develop the mood
- Mentions vivid vocabulary but does not give examples
- References are more than brief but less than insightful. Some connections are made between literary elements.

Theme: 3
- Mentions two themes
- Themes are briefly mentioned without details or explanation.

Interpretation: 5
- Shows literal understanding and then moves beyond to symbolic
- Shows understanding of the symbolism of the leaf and feather at the end of the story
- Evaluates characters, their feelings, and motives
- Evaluates the story's ending
- Makes predictions about the future of the characters
- Interpretations are original and not immediately obvious in the story.

Making Connections: 4
- Compares to fairy tale genre
- Makes connections to "The Little Mermaid"
- Compares to own life by wanting to be unselfish like the protagonist
- Explains relevant personal and literary connections, but they do not add greatly to the meaning of the text.

Response Example 2

I think the idea of an old lonely man was great. You could almost feel his sorrow and loneliness. It's sad the way it ended, him without a wife, but he did not seem lonely by any means. The author gave great description of the setting and the characters. I think he wished for himself to die but to still be with his swan wife.

I think the story began pretty good, him finding the swan and saving it. I also think the climax was when he was deciding whether to turn his wife back into a swan or turn her sister human. It was neat the way he said he was not going to use his last wish.

The theme I'm not quite sure about, but I think the author's message is that you shouldn't change people's (or animal's) appearance. Or you should be happy with what you have. Maybe he should have rejected the three wishes. Of course, that's almost impossible for any human I know.

Overall, I think this is a wonderful story and would like to read it again.

Analysis of Response Example 2 (Using the Rubric)

Literary Elements: 2

- More than just a summary (with plot, characters and climax mentioned) but does not expand on ideas.

Theme: 3

- The two themes mentioned are brief and superficial, not detailed.

Interpretation: 1

- Attempts interpretation but does not explain or support ideas. Therefore the interpretation is confusing, unfounded, and unclear. A literal interpretation of the story is not apparent.

Making Connections: 2

- Makes a generalization about human nature and connects it to the story. This connection is brief and unsupported.

Selecting and Introducing Short Stories

The teacher should select short stories based upon the reading level of the students. The stories should appeal to a wide variety of interests and should include several different genres. As with the poetry, the teacher should enthusiastically introduce each of the short stories, allow students to make their first, second, and third choice of which story to read, and make groups accordingly. If a student did not get his/her first choice in either of the poetry rounds, it is very important to give him/her a first choice during the short story portion of the literature circles program. The teacher might begin like this:

> Students, we are now beginning our short stories round of the Literature Circles program. If you did not receive your first choice during the poetry round please remind me so that I can make sure to give you your first choice of stories. I have six wonderful short stories to introduce to you. The first one is "The Bracelet" by Yoshiko Uchida. This story has a great theme of friendship, and it takes place during World War II when Japanese Americans were sent away to internment camps. If you like historical fiction and stories about injustice, then this story is definitely one you will enjoy.

> [The teacher goes on to introduce all stories and students make their choices.]

Student Responsibilities
As with the poetry phase, students are responsible for reading the material thoroughly, making margin notes as they read, and completing a pre-discussion response in their journals before their meeting date. Students should also be using their rubrics when formulating their responses. Students must bring their text and journals with them to the meetings.

Responding to Short Stories

Students need to be reminded that short story responses (pre-discussion) will be different from poetry responses. Short story responses should be longer (two pages is recommended) and must include discussion of elements not present in poetry. Before students begin their responses, teachers should use "Suggested Ways to Respond to Short Stories" (see page 81) either as a handout or overhead transparency to explain how to respond to short stories. See pages 82–83 for examples of margin notes and page 84 for a sample pre-discussion response.

Suggested Ways to Respond to Short Stories

Pre-discussion response (2 pages):

1. Begin with a one-paragraph summary about the story.

2. Read through the reading rubric and "Topics for Pre-Discussion Journal Responses" to ensure that you cover all important aspects of short stories.

3. Be sure to include literary elements and how they interact.
   Examples:
   How does the setting create a mood for the story?
   How does the conflict affect (and change) the characters?

4. Save your evaluation of the story until the end of your response.

5. Be sure to support your ideas with quotes from the story.

Response to an excerpt from "The Bracelet" by Yoshiko Uchida

The Bracelet
Yoshiko Uchida

Where are they going?

Emi didn't want her big sister to see her cry. She wiped the tears away quickly, but couldn't wipe away the sadness inside.

"It's almost time to go," her mother called.

And Emi knew they would have to leave their home soon.

She looked around her room. It was as empty now as the rest of the house. Like a gift box with no gift inside—filled with a lot of nothing.

Great simile. Really shows emptiness.

This sounds very serious.

Emi closed her eyes and tried to remember how it had looked. Flowered chintz curtains at the window, her clothes scattered everywhere, her favorite rag doll and teddy bear sitting on the chest.

She could even remember how the whole house looked if she closed her eyes and kept pictures of it inside her head.

Emi and her family weren't moving because they wanted to. The government was sending them to a prison camp because they were Japanese-Americans. And America was at war with Japan.

This does not seem fair.

They hadn't done anything wrong. They were being treated like the enemy just because they *looked* like the enemy. The FBI had sent Papa to a prisoner-of-war camp in Montana just because he worked for a Japanese company.

It was crazy, Emi thought. They loved America, but America didn't love them back. And it didn't want to trust them.

Emi ran to the door when she heard the doorbell. Maybe, she thought, a messenger from the government would be standing there, tall and proper and buttoned into a uniform. Maybe he would tell them it was all a mistake, that they didn't have to go to camp after all.

I don't think this will happen.

But when Emi opened the door, it wasn't a messenger at all. It was her best friend, Laurie Madison.... She came with a gift, as though she'd come for a birthday party. But she wasn't wearing her good party dress, and she looked just as sad as Emi felt.

"Here," she said, thrusting her gift at Emi. "It's a bracelet. It's for you to take to camp."

Shows some tension.

Laurie helped Emi put on the bracelet. It was a thin gold chain with a heart dangling from it, and Emi loved it the minute she saw it.

"I'll never take it off," Emi promised. "Not even when I take a shower."

Laurie gave Emi a hug. "Well, good-bye, then," she said. "Come back soon."

"I will," Emi answered. But she really didn't know if she'd ever come back to Berkeley. Maybe she would never see Laurie again.

She watched as Laurie walked down the block, turning and waving and walking backwards until she got to the corner.

Emi couldn't bear to watch anymore, and she slammed the door shut.

This is so sad. I can't imagine this happening to me.

When the doorbell rang again, it was their neighbor, Mrs. Simpson. She'd come to take them to the center where all the Japanese-Americans were to report.

I wonder how Mrs. Simpson feels about all of this.

"Come on, Emi. Get your things," her sister, Reiko, called. "It's time to go."

Emi made sure her gold bracelet was secure on her wrist. Then she put on both her sweater and her coat so she wouldn't have to carry them. They could take only what they could carry, and her two suitcases were already full. Each family had a number now, and Emi put tags with their number, 13453, on her two suitcases.

They have numbers— like animals?

Mama took a last look around the house, going from room to room. Emi followed her, trying to remember how each one had looked when they were filled with furniture and rugs and pictures and books.

They went out for a last look at the garden Papa loved. If he were here now, Emi knew he would pick one of the prettiest carnations and bring it inside. "This is for you, Mama," he would say, and Mama would smile and put it in her best crystal vase.

She must really miss her father.

But now the garden looked shabby and bare. Papa was gone and Mama was too busy to care for it. It looked the way Emi felt—lonely and abandoned.

Great description here—shows the sadness.

Sample Student Pre-Discussion Journal Response

The following is a pre-discussion response to "The Bracelet" by Yoshiko Uchida.

During World War II, Emi, her mom, and her sister were sent to a relocation center because they were Japanese. The FBI had already taken their father away. Right before Emi left, her best friend, Laurie, stopped by to give her a good-bye present. Emi opened it to find a gold bracelet with a heart dangling from it. Emi said she would never take it off, and with that Laurie sadly walked away. When Emi arrived at the camp, she was excited about having an apartment, but to her dismay she found her apartment was only a stall which had housed a racehorse. (The camp used to be a horseracing track.) As soon as the family had unpacked, Emi realized she had lost her bracelet from Laurie. She looked everywhere and never found it. She learned that the bracelet was only a symbol of her friendship with Laurie, and that friendship is always carried in the heart.

The tone in this story really impacts the mood. The author's attitude toward the events is very sad which makes the mood of the story very sad too. The setting also helps to show the mood. This quote is a great example, "It was as empty now as the rest of the house. Like a gift box with no gift inside—filled with a lot of nothing." This is also a good example of a simile. Later in the story, the vivid description of the camp makes the mood even more depressing.

The conflict of this story (the family having to leave their home to go to an internment camp) makes the reader think how cruel people can be to their own citizens.

I think that the author's theme was that an object can't make a friendship last. It is the friendship that you share that is important. Also, there was a theme of prejudice. It is hard to believe what prejudice can cause people to do. Innocent people were forced to leave their own houses and not see their friends, just because of the way they looked and because their ancestors were Japanese.

This short story was very strong and moving. It went to my heart that the United States would do such a terrible thing to their own citizens. It was very untrusting of us.

Group Meetings

For the first round of short stories, the teacher should again meet with each group individually. Teachers can proceed as they did with poetry, by acting as guides, not leaders. Teachers should ensure that students have read and understood the story, and that discussions take into account the different elements present in short stories (such as conflict, climax, resolution, and sentence variety) while still responding to the figurative language and personal/literary connections.

Sample Student Discussion

The following is an excerpt from a group discussion of "The Bracelet."

Student 1: This was a very sad story about how we treated the Japanese during World War II.

Student 2: Yes, but why was it called "The Bracelet"? It seemed like the bracelet was not the main point of the story.

Student 3: I thought that the bracelet symbolized the friendship between Laurie and Emi and that is why it was the title of the story.

Student 1: Yes, the theme of the story was definitely friendship.

Student 2: I don't think that was the theme. I thought it was more about prejudice and treating people unfairly.

Teacher: In any story, there can be more than one theme. Often authors have many themes they are trying to convey. I think this is one of those times. Both of you are correct in themes that you see present.

Student 4: I didn't like that the characters weren't very well described. I felt like I couldn't picture the characters very well except maybe for Laurie. I wanted more details.

Student 3: I agree. I liked the story, but I couldn't really picture the people. The setting was very well described though.

Student 2: You know, I just remembered a book I read called *Escape from Warsaw*. It had some similarities to this story, because it was also about World War II and how unfairly people were treated in Europe.

Sample Student Post-Discussion Journal Response

After students finish their discussion, they should write a one page post-discussion response. The following is an example regarding "The Bracelet."

During my group discussion we talked about the characters and their personalities, the mood, and we compared this story to other literature we read.

For the characters, we were able to figure out that Mama was a brave and strong person. Emi, the main character, seemed to have high respect for her sister and had a great friendship with Laurie. Laurie was a polite girl and seemed to be generous. The Papa of Emi worked for an engineering company and was sent to a separate relocation center. He loved to garden and loved his family. Emi's older sister was stern and sometimes wise.

This short story reminded me of a story I read a few months ago. I did not remember this until the discussion. The book was called *Escape from Warsaw* by Ian Serralier. The father was Polish and was sent to a concentration camp early in the year for turning a picture of Hitler toward the wall. The mother was taken away to another concentration camp. The family had a plan to meet in Switzerland if they were ever separated. The family was reunited at the end. Both stories took place during World War Two and really clearly showed what happens to families during times of war. Innocent people went through many hardships because of war and politics.

We also discussed our opinions about the story. Jonathan thought the ending was tacked on and it bothered him. And after thinking about it, I agreed with him. It did need a better closure. Katie thought that only the beginning and the end talked about the story and the end of the story talked about the bracelet, and the story should have had more on that subject. I really disagree, because it was important in the middle of the story to talk about the horrible conditions of the relocation center. Otherwise, you would not have understood how painful it must have been to have to live in a camp.

I also think that Uchida should have showed more emotions in her characters. Most of the emotions were explained rather than showed. We all agreed that the author could have described the appearance of the characters also. The only character who was described was Laurie, and it only said that "she wasn't wearing a party dress."

When we talked about the mood, we all agreed that it was sad, and the tone was about unfairness.

I thought that our discussion went well, and that all members had a chance to share their ideas and questions.

Evaluating Group Discussions

It is important, before the next round of short stories, to conduct a whole class discussion to evaluate the progress of the literature circles discussions. The teacher and students can brainstorm a list of discussion strengths as well as a list of possible improvements. The teacher might say:

> Now it is time to think about how our discussions are progressing. Right now on a piece of binder paper, I want you to brainstorm three strengths that your discussions groups have had, and three areas that need improvement. We will share those ideas, and brainstorm how to achieve improvement in the weak areas.

Some sample strengths:

1. Good eye contact during discussions.

2. People are prepared for discussions.

3. People are taking the discussions seriously.

4. People are demonstrating active listening.

Some sample weaknesses and methods for improvement:

1. Some people are not participating in discussion.

   Solution: Group members can ask polite questions of those students, such as "Michael, what is your favorite poem?" or "John, what did you think the theme of this story was?"

2. Some people are dominating the discussion.

   Solution: Assign one group member the role of facilitator in order to move the discussion along. "Elizabeth, thank you for your ideas, but we need to ask other group members what they think." "Josh, can you talk more slowly and give other people a chance to respond to your ideas?"

3. Some people are getting the discussion off topic.

   Solution: The class can develop a signal when someone is discussing irrelevant matters. For example, if a student is getting off the subject, without interrupting the student other group members can point to the literature to let the person know.

This list of problems and solutions should be posted in the classroom so that students will keep these ideas in mind for future discussions.

Second Round of Short Stories

Before forming new groups, teachers can reintroduce the stories or previous groups can be responsible for presenting and recommending the stories. New groups are formed, the class members are given their new short stories, and they begin preparations for their next group meetings.

Simultaneous Group Meetings

After two rounds of poetry and one round of short stories, the students should be ready to meet on their own without the teacher present for the entire discussion. Students need to know that they will still be accountable for preparedness and participation even though the teacher will not be present at all times.

Before the groups meet simultaneously, the teacher should review the rules. At this point, it is recommended that the class create a "I should see, I should hear" chart regarding literature circles behaviors. Some examples for "I should see" might include eye contact, people facing each other, active participation and listening, and all materials out and being used. Some examples for "I should hear" might include one voice at a time, sharing of ideas, questions, and participation of all members.

There are three options for teachers regarding evaluation of simultaneous group meetings. Teachers can tape record groups and listen to discussions at a later time. Teachers can circulate throughout the room and take anecdotal records of discussions. Lastly, students can and should evaluate their group members using "Evaluate Your Literature Circles Group" on page 89.

Evaluating Journals

The journals can now be evaluated by the teacher using the rubric. Teachers can decide if they want to evaluate the journals after each round of short stories or at the end of both rounds. This will depend upon the progress of the students and their need for feedback. Students can also evaluate their own journals using the rubric.

Projects

Now that students have completed the short story and poetry phases of literature circles, it is time to move on to novels. However, students have been working at a very fast pace up to this point. This is a good time to slow things down a bit and work on some projects to wrap up the progress so far. Some examples for projects are presented on page 90.

Evaluate Your Literature Circles Group

Give each member of your literature circles group a grade for his/her participation in the discussion. Use the rubric below in determining the grade.

Check Plus

☐ Brought text and journal to the discussion.

☐ Contributed often and initiated topics of discussion.

☐ Comments were relevant, insightful, and increased the group's understanding of the material.

☐ Referred to the text often during the discussion.

☐ Listened actively and responded to others without interrupting.

Check

☐ Brought text and journal to the discussion.

☐ Contributed occasionally.

☐ Comments were usually relevant and meaningful.

☐ Referred to the text occasionally during the discussion.

☐ Listened and occasionally responded to others.

☐ May have interrupted other students occasionally.

Check Minus

☐ Some materials may have been missing.

☐ Rarely or never contributed.

☐ Comments may have been off topic.

☐ Did not refer to text during discussion.

☐ Listened, but rarely responded unless asked directly.

☐ May not have paid attention during the discussion or often interrupted other students.

Name	Score
1. _____	_____
2. _____	_____
3. _____	_____
4. _____	_____
5. _____	_____
6. _____	_____

Poetry and Short Story Projects

1. Choose a favorite poem. Rewrite it in another style and change it to make it "yours." Or choose a favorite poet and write a poem imitating his/her style.

2. Choose a favorite poem. Write it out on art paper and illustrate.

3. Rewrite one of the short stories you read. Change the ending, add or delete characters, or turn it into a play or poem.

4. Choose a favorite author out of the poems or short stories read so far. Research information about his or her background, education, family, and other literature published. Create a poster about the author explaining the facts you learned.

5. Choose a favorite passage from one of the short stories you read. This should be a descriptive or pivotal passage from the story. Write the passage out on art paper and illustrate it.

6. Create a "Citizen of the Decade" award for one of the characters in a short story you have read. Use the format shown below, or make up your own.

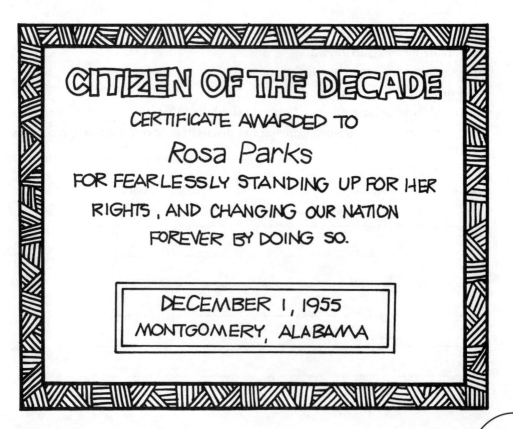

CITIZEN OF THE DECADE

CERTIFICATE AWARDED TO

Rosa Parks

FOR FEARLESSLY STANDING UP FOR HER RIGHTS, AND CHANGING OUR NATION FOREVER BY DOING SO.

DECEMBER 1, 1955
MONTGOMERY, ALABAMA

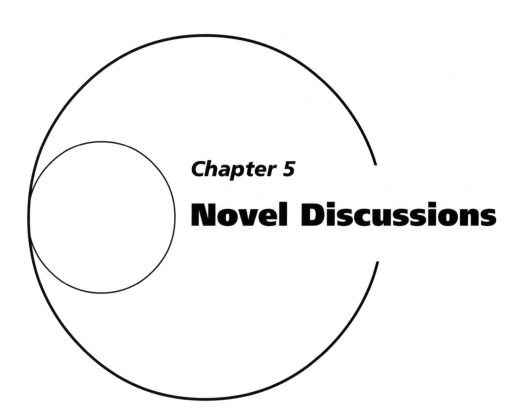

Chapter 5

Novel Discussions

Getting Started With Novels

Now that students are experienced at literature circles, it is time to approach the novel. Before beginning the novel selection, it is recommended that teachers take the time to evaluate the program's success so far.

- How are the students responding to the literature?
- How are they progressing in their journals and discussions?
- Are there any behavior problems that are becoming a distraction?
- Are the students stretching their minds and taking chances in their interpretations, or are they falling into a rut of safe, narrow discussions?

If there are any problems, teachers should stop and rectify them before moving ahead. It might be a good time for a mini-lesson on theme, symbolism, or plot development. Perhaps students just need a day to organize their journals and reflect on what they have learned so far. Regardless of the problem, before beginning the novel, teachers should slow down a bit to evaluate the program's progress.

Choosing Novels and Making Groups

Once teachers have ascertained that everything is going smoothly, students need to be introduced to their choices of novels. Depending upon the class size and ability range, teachers should choose between four to seven novels to introduce. These novels should be varied in their reading level, genre, and theme. In addition, teachers must be careful to avoid choosing novels that will divide the class by race or gender.

When forming groups for novel discussions, teachers must select students very carefully. At this point, teachers should know how well their groups are working. Novel groups will meet at least four times to discuss the book. Therefore it is very important that the groups be balanced in ability level and also in personality and behavior components. Because the novel groups will work so closely together, it is crucial that all students can work with their group members to achieve their maximum potential. If teachers have previously established cooperative learning rules in their classroom, this would be an appropriate time to reinforce those rules to ensure that all students are comfortable with their group members. Teachers must also reinforce participation rules for talking and for listening.

Literature Circles Novel Contract

Once students have been told which novel they are going to read, it is recommended that they fill out a contract regarding responsibility of the book. Literature circles novels must be partially read at home. Therefore, unless the students purchase their own books, they must be held responsible for the care of the book. In addition, all students must be held responsible for completing the required reading by the assigned time. It is imperative that students complete their reading in time for discussion; otherwise the group cannot function in a way that is beneficial for all members. See page 93 for a contract example. Students must have the contract signed, by themselves and their parent/guardian, before they are allowed to take a copy of the book home. Even if they do purchase their own copy, they still must sign the contract in regard to completing the assigned reading.

Name: _____

Literature Circles Novel Contract

Title of Book: _____

Number of Book: _____

1. If I am borrowing the teacher's book or the school's book, it is my responsibility to keep the book in good condition. If I lose or damage the book in any way, it is my responsibility to *buy* a replacement copy.

2. I will bring the book with me to school every day.

3. I will have the assigned chapters read by the assigned dates.

_____   _____
Student Signature   Parent/Guardian Signature

Using Sticky Notes

In responding to poetry and short stories, it was recommended that students make comments directly on the literature, and then transfer those comments into their journals. Unfortunately, unless students purchase their own books, it is not possible for them to write in their novels. In order to work around this impediment, it is recommended that students be trained to use sticky notes to record their pre-discussion impressions. These notes can be used whenever a thought, question, connection, or observation is made by the student, and can then be placed into the book at the appropriate place, as shown on pages 95–97. This makes it very easy for students during discussions, as they can refer to their books when making a point. Teachers can accept the sticky notes as the pre-discussion response, or the students can use those notes to formulate a more organized response prior to discussion. If students use sticky notes as their pre-discussion response, they should place them on binder paper with a page number on each sticky note. The sticky notes should not be removed from the novel until after students have had their discussions.

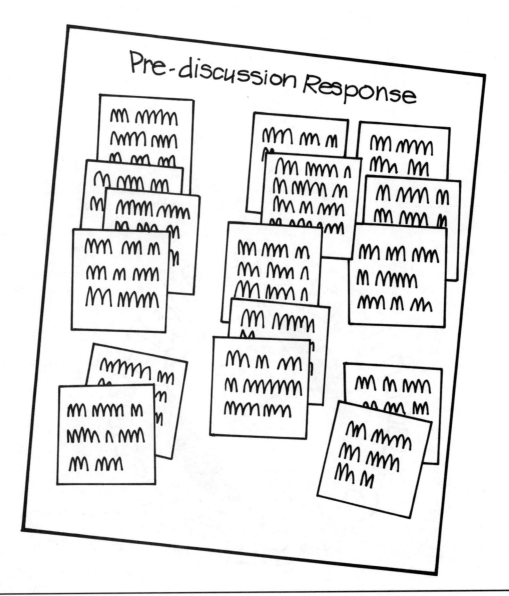

Examples of Responses to Literature Using Sticky Notes

Excerpts from *That Was Then, This Is Now* by S.E. Hinton

When this chick and me broke up, I still stayed friends with her brother, which is unusual in cases like that. Charlie, the bartender, was just ___ t he had a tough reputation and kept order real good. We ___ art of town and some pretty wild things went on in C ___

I looked around for a plainclothes cop when ___ s tell a cop—but didn't find one, so I went up to the ba ___

"Give me a beer," I said, and Charlie, who w ___ e every bartender you ever see, gave me a dirty look inst ___ ly, "a Coke."

"Your credit ain't so hot, Bryon," Charlie sai ___ "A dime—for cryin' out loud! Can't you let me charge a dime Coke?"

"Cokes are fifteen cents, and you already got three dollars worth of Cokes charged here, and if you don't pay up this month, I'll have to beat it out of you." He said this real friendly-like, but he meant it. We were friends, but Charlie was a businessman too.

"I'll pay up," I assured him. "Don't worry."

Charlie gave me a lopsided grin. "I ain't worried, kid. You're the one who should be worried."

> **Why is there so much slang and bad grammar in this book?**

That bugged the heck out of me. Mark was ___ that. I ought to know. Mark had lived at my house ever ___ s nine and his parents shot each other in a drunken argu ___ sorry for him and took him home to live with us. My mo ___ ds and could only have one, so until she got hold of Ma ___ feeding every stray cat that came along. There was no te ___ might have picked up along the line if she could have ___ me and Mark.

> **Here's the theme—Friendship! They will always be friends even though they have hard times!**

I had been friends w ___ came to live with us. He had lived down the street and ___ ad always been together. We had never had a fight. W ___ rgument. In looks, we were complete opposites: I'm a big ___ he kind who looks like a Saint Bernard puppy, whic ___ icks cannot resist a Saint Bernard puppy. Mark was sm ___ nge golden eyes and hair to match and a grin like a frien ___ onger than he looked—he could tie me in arm wrestling. ___ d we were like brothers.

> **I like the description here—good simile (St. Bernard puppy)**
>
> **The kids sound really tough— is it an act or for real?**

Mark could hot-wire anything, and [ ] years old he had hot-wired cars and driven them. He had [ ] ut he finally got caught at it, so now once a week h[ ] his school lunch hour to see his probation officer and tell [ ] bing to steal cars anymore. I had been worried at fir[ ] to take Mark and put him in a boys' home since he wasr[ ] didn't have a family. I was worried about Mark being lo[ ] Mark always came through everything untouched, ur[ ]

> *Mark sounds like his luck will run out someday. I don't know if I like his character. He's too shady and tough.*

Mike paused here for a minute. He was staring off in the distance, and when he started talking again, it was slowly, like he was living the whole thing over again.

The big guy came around to my side of the car. "You hurt her, white boy?"

"No," I said, and it didn't sound very loud so I cleared my throat and said, "No, I didn't," so loud that it sounded like I was sh[ ]uting. It was real quiet; you could hear somebody's TV from down [ ] dog barking a block away and Connie's soft sobbing. I [ ] ounding in my ears. Then the big guy said really quiet-[ ] eve you?" And I got so scared I was about to cry and [ ] k her!" The guy called across the car, "Connie, what [ ] s white cat?"

"And real soft—her voice w[ ]—she said, "Kill the white bastard."

"And sure enough, they almo[ ]

> *What an awful story. What is the point of this story? Is it hinting about things to come?*
>
> *Something bad is on the way.*

This was wrong. For the first time in years I th_____ __ __out the golden-eyed
cowboy who had been Mark's ___ _____ ____ _ ____ _yback? To what? I
wondered tiredly why I had ne__ _____ ___ __ ad absolutely no concept
of what was right and what wa_ _____ _ __ __ ny laws, because he
couldn't see that there were any_ _____ ____ __ they didn't matter to
Mark, because they were just w____ ___ ___ ___

"Bryon, what is it?" Mark c____ ___ _____ ___ __ t bugs you that much I'll
quit. I'll stop selling if you don't ____ ___ ___ ught it would bother you.
I sort of thought you knew abou_ ___ _____

Don't drag me into this, I tho____ ___ ___ ___ ne out to be blind, just
because you are. Aloud I said, "I____ ___ ____ _t as if I was talking in
my sleep. Mark went white.

> *I can't believe he turned Mark in. I don't think he should have. He should have asked Mark first, but he was too upset about M + M.*

The police arrived, and of co__ ___ ___ ___ idn't know what was going
on. She could only stand hel_ ___ ___ ___ ay while the police
questioned me, rounded up ___ ___ ___ ___ ndcuffs on Mark. They
advised Mark of his right to ___ ___ ___ _. He just stood there,
quivering, watching me wh___ ___ ___ gs that would put him behind
bars for years.

Then a cop said, "Let'_ ___ ___ ___ to dawn on Mark what was
happening. He looked qu___ ___ ___ and cried, "My God, Bryon,
you're not gonna let the__ ___

> *I think S.E. Hinton wrote this book to show how tough life is for teens and how many choices kids make.*

What if I hadn't met her in the first place, would I still have grown away from
Mark? W___ ___ ___ ___ good trip instead of a bad one? What if someone
else had ___ ___ ___ there still be hope for him?

I am ___ ___ ___ are. And to think, I used to be sure of things. Me,
once I h___ ___ ___ I was a kid again, when I had all the answers.

> *The end of the book is so sad. I don't like it! I like happy endings.*
>
> *This was too realistic and depressing.*

First Group Meeting and Subsequent Scheduling

Scheduling for novel completion is one more aspect of literature circles that is left up to the students. After students have been given their novels, teachers should set up the first meeting, giving all students an assignment to have completed by that time. (For example, students should read chapters one and two for the first discussion.) Students can be given time in class to complete the reading, and to prepare their responses for discussion, or the reading and responses can be assigned for homework.

Depending upon the prior achievement of the students during the poetry and short story phases of literature circles, teachers need to decide upon the structure for the first novel meeting. If necessary, teachers can schedule the meetings so that each group meets individually with teacher supervision or input. Ideally, groups should be functioning well enough for simultaneous meetings to occur, with limited teacher involvement. This gives the literature circles program greater flexibility and gives the students independence and self-motivation.

At the first meeting, discussions should revolve around the first few chapters of the book. It is important for students to make predictions at this point as well, something that was not possible during prior stages of the literature circles program. Teachers should be careful not to lead discussions as they move from group to group, but should point out differences in discussing a novel and give groups some guidance in how to direct their discussions. Students should be contemplating characters, episodes, plot, theme or themes, genre, suspense, point of view, and the author's style.

Student Discussion Example

The following is an excerpt of a student discussion of the novel, *That Was Then, This Is Now* by S.E. Hinton.

> **Student 1**: I like this book so far. It seems really realistic, and the characters seem like regular teenagers.
>
> **Student 2**: Yeah, but why do they use such weird words and slang?
>
> **Student 3**: Well, don't forget that this was written a long time ago.
>
> **Student 2**: When was it written? Let's look. Oh, it was written in 1971. No wonder things sound different.
>
> **Student 1**: In the 1970s there were hippies and stuff. So that must be why M&M is so strange.
>
> **Student 4**: These kids have really difficult lives. Can you believe that Mark's parents shot each other? What a horrible experience for him.
>
> **Student 1**: And they hang out at a bar. I don't think kids can do that now, but maybe in the 70s it was OK for kids to drink.
>
> **Student 4**: What do you think is going to happen to these kids. I mean, bad things have already happened, like that story about the black girl, Connie. But it seems like something even worse might happen. I wonder what it will be? Because you know that books always have to have a conflict.
>
> **Student 3**: Yeah, that story might be foreshadowing a conflict that will happen later on.
>
> **Student 2**: Well, I hope that nothing bad happens to M&M. He seems so sweet and innocent.

Students continue their discussion until they have covered all the topics they feel need to be explained. After students complete their first discussion, before breaking to work independently on their post-discussion responses, the groups need to decide upon their schedule for completing the book. All students will complete their books on the same, prearranged day. However, it is up to each individual group to decide how much will be read before meetings two, three, and four (the dates for which have been predetermined by the teacher). See "Literature Circles Schedule" on page 100 for an example. Teachers should ensure that all groups are in agreement on the scheduling and keep a copy of each group's schedule. If students make unrealistic deadlines for completion of their reading, teachers should intervene.

Literature Circles Schedule

Title of Novel: _____

	Date	Chapters to Read Before Discussion

Meeting 1: _____   Chapters: _____

Meeting 2: _____   Chapters: _____

Meeting 3: _____   Chapters: _____

Meeting 4: _____   The entire book will be completed.

Evaluating Students

Students will meet four times to discuss their novels. During each meeting, students will discuss their journal responses and/or sticky notes. Teachers will monitor meetings and sit in with groups, evaluating group participation, and individual member's contributions. Teachers must also evaluate journals. It is recommended that teachers not wait until the novel is completed to evaluate the students' journal responses. Although students should be experts in their journals at this point, responding to novels is often more complex than responding to poems or short stories. There is just a lot more to think about. Teachers should evaluate journals after the first meeting in order to gauge how students are progressing. If necessary, and depending upon how much prior novel work students have done, the teacher can then intersperse literature circles with some mini-lessons about interpreting a novel. Students might not need this extra information, but it is important for teachers to make that decision based upon their evaluation of the student journals. Some sample lessons may include the following:

1. Making predictions about future events and using foreshadowing.

2. Identifying episodes within a book and evaluating how they add to the plot.

3. Identifying major plots and subplots.

4. Analyzing characters and their development.

5. Comparing and contrasting characters.

6. Identifying and analyzing themes.

7. Evaluating the writer's style.

Assigning Book Projects

Once novels have been completed and students have finished their discussions, it is up to the teacher to decide about assigning a final book project. If students are going to complete another novel, this is a good way to remind them about the choices they have for their second round. See "Final Book Project" guidelines and suggestions on page 102 for a sample culminating book project.

THE SECRET GARDEN • BURNETT

Final Book Project

In this project, your group is going to present your literature circles book to the rest of the class in such a way that they will want to read it.

Guidelines

1. Your presentation must be 3–5 minutes.

2. Everyone in your group must speak and participate in the presentation.

3. You must try to "sell" the book or make it sound appealing. You are recommending the book for others to read.

4. Do not give away crucial facts or the ending! Leave some suspense for future readers.

Suggestions

You may choose one of these suggestions, or you may create your own project. You also have the option of combining ideas. You must have your ideas approved by the teacher before beginning your project, and all group members must agree on the project choice.

1. Choose a scene from the book and act it out.

2. Make a poster or visual aid to explain your book.

3. Summarize the book in any form (play, poetry, etc.).

4. Make a book map explaining the plot, setting, or both.

5. Pretend you are characters in the novel. Take on the characters' dialects and mannerisms. Explain to the class who you are and how you fit into the plot of the book.

6. Read some particularly interesting passages aloud—dramatically.

7. Make a commercial for the book. This can be a magazine, radio, or television advertisement.

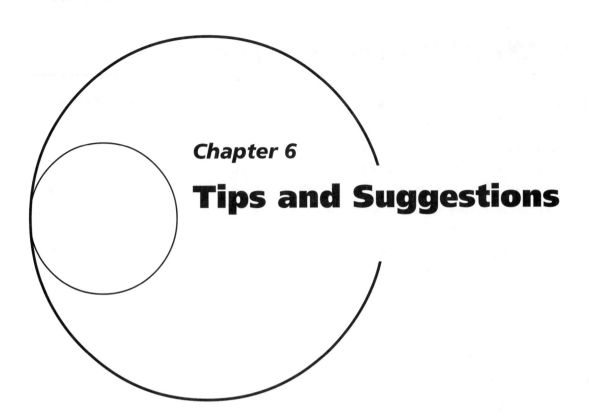

Chapter 6

Tips and Suggestions

Tips and Suggestions

This chapter offers tips and suggestions for teachers regarding common problems and questions that may come up during literature circles, and gives solutions and answers.

Journal Problems

It is important that students keep their journals organized, complete, and neat during literature circles, as the journal is a large component of their grade and a major indicator of their growth. Teachers must collect and evaluate journals on a regular basis to ensure that students' journals are up to class standards and are being used correctly. If at any time the teacher notices that a large percentage of journals is not meeting the standards set, it is a good idea to stop literature circles temporarily in order to reteach proper journal format and journal expectations.

Students need to know that they are expected to put much thought and detail into their responses. It is always a good idea to go through the suggested topics list and do mini-lessons regarding those literary elements. In this way, students will know that merely summarizing the literature in their journals is not adequate.

Once students have been trained to use the high-level comprehension rubric, they can be held responsible for evaluating their own journal responses. In addition, students can trade and evaluate each other's journals if the teacher feels it is appropriate. This will ensure that students are receiving significant feedback on their journal responses.

Discussion Problems

Discussions are the crux of the literature circles program, as these are where ideas are exchanged and new learning occurs. It is of paramount importance that these discussions run smoothly, without any behavior or participation problems. For the first three rounds of literature circles, teachers must sit with each group individually to prevent behavior problems before they start, to model questions and discussion strategies, and to ensure that all students are participating equally. This strategy will prevent most problems from ever occurring.

If groups are having discussion problems when the groups are meeting simultaneously, teachers have a few different options:

1. Teachers can tape record group discussions so that students are held accountable for their participation and behavior.

2. Students can evaluate their group and add detailed comments about problems.

3. Groups do not have to meet simultaneously. If necessary, the teacher can continue to hold discussions with each individual group and monitor those discussions closely.

4. If only one group is having problems, the teacher can sit with that group while other groups are meeting.

5. There are many lessons and books available regarding cooperative learning and working collaboratively. The teacher may want to incorporate some cooperative lessons into the curriculum. Students can role-play different group situations and work together to form solutions.

Students Who Are Not Prepared

In an ideal situation, all students would have their reading and journal responses completed prior to every discussion. In the literature circles program, because students have choice in their reading and responses, there will be a high percentage of students who have completed their work. However, as in any classroom situation, there are always some students who are not prepared for their discussions.

Teachers need to decide upon their own grading systems (regarding late and missing work). However, discussions should be a major component of a student's literature circles grade. Participating in a discussion with peers is fun and a privilege. If students are not prepared for their discussion, it is recommended that they do not participate. Instead, they should be given a chance to finish their work while their group is holding their discussion. It is then their responsibility to discuss the reading with group members on their own time (this is also a good strategy for students who are absent). If a large percentage of students is not prepared for discussion, the teacher may not be giving enough class time for students to work.

From the start of literature circles, teachers must prepare their students for success. This involves giving ample class time for students to read and respond (especially in the beginning when students have many questions), and it entails much teacher involvement in the discussions during the beginning of the program.

Student Measurement

It is important for teachers to know if their students made progress during literature circles. This will help teachers in their planning for the next round of literature circles, by letting them know if there are any areas of weakness which might necessitate reteaching or mini-lessons.

In order to measure growth, teachers can administer a pre- and post-literature test. The test should be something simple, such as an unguided response to a story. The teacher can choose two short stories (one for the pretest and one for the posttest) and ask a question such as "Please respond to the story with your thoughts, feelings, ideas, and questions. As you respond, think about the literary elements, the theme, your interpretation of the story, and connections to your life and/or other literature." These responses can then be evaluated using the high-level comprehension rubric.

Although literature circles does not focus on traditional standardized test types of questions, it is possible to gauge student growth by using standardized tests. Literature circles, when done correctly by the student, will raise a student's reading comprehension. Therefore the teacher can compare the current year's test with tests from previous years to measure student reading gains.

Scheduling: What Does the Program Look Like?

The literature circles program is flexible enough to fit into any type of time schedule. It is easiest to schedule when teachers have a large block of time set aside for English, but it can also work in a one period English class. Much of the reading and responding can be done for homework if necessary, so that the majority of class time can be used for group discussions.

A typical day in the classroom might look like this:

9:00–9:30   Read poems individually and work on responses.

9:30–9:45   One group will meet with the teacher for discussion. Other students finish their responses and work on other activities (see "Rules for Discussions" handout on page 39).

9:45–10:00   Another group will meet with the teacher for discussion. Other students finish their responses and work on other activities (see "Rules for Discussions" handout on page 39).

10:00   Class is over, or students work on other lessons as a whole class.

Parent/Guardian Involvement and Evaluation of the Program

It is important for parents to understand the literature circles program, how it works, and why it is being implemented. Teachers may want to send a letter home at the beginning of the program explaining to parents the new requirements that students must meet. Parents should be aware that their children will be concentrating heavily on reading, and it would be very beneficial for parents to discuss that reading with their children. A sample letter that the authors sent to all parents/guardians prior to beginning literature circles is given on page 107.

Literature Circles Information
for Parents/Guardians

Dear Parents/Guardians,

We will be starting a new type of reading curriculum in our classrooms at the beginning of next month. This change is an exciting one, as it will allow your children to select the literature they will read (from choices we give them), and they will then meet in small groups for thorough discussion of the literature. This reading program is called "Literature Circles," and it will help your child to improve reading comprehension.

Literature Circles improves comprehension in a number of ways:

1. Students read literature they have selected, which means that they are interested and motivated to read.
2. Students respond to the literature by writing pre-discussion and post-discussion responses. Any ideas, comments, questions, and thoughts they have will be thoroughly discussed in a group meeting.
3. Students discuss the literature thoroughly with their peers (with teacher supervision). All students must participate, so that all voices are heard. Students can have all of their questions answered and can share their ideas.
4. Literature Circles guarantees that students will have active involvement with their literature. In addition, they develop better communication skills as they meet and discuss with their peers.

During the Literature Circles program, your child will have a few responsibilities that are new. We would appreciate your input in ensuring that your child is prepared for this new program.

1. Your child needs to purchase a report folder or binder to use as a literature circles journal. This folder will be kept in class. Your child should bring this folder to class by: _____ .
2. During literature circles meetings, your child must be involved and must participate. It would be helpful if you, as parents, could discuss the literature with your child prior to meetings. This will help immensely to ensure that your child is prepared for discussion.
3. When your child is not meeting with his or her group, he or she must be involved in a quiet classroom activity. These will be explained by the teacher, but if your child does not cooperate, there will be consequences. We would appreciate it if you would emphasize to your child how important good behavior is during literature circles.

Thank you for your time and cooperation. We know your child will benefit from Literature Circles. We are excited about starting this new program, and we welcome any input you might have.

Sincerely,

_____ DATE: _____

Student and Parent/Guardian Evaluation

In addition to other forms of evaluation, students should reflect upon their learning during literature circles. Self-evaluation is a critical part of the learning process. It is therefore recommended that students and parents/guardians evaluate the program, its benefits, and what was learned. A "Student and Parent/Guardian Evaluation of Literature Circles" is included on pages 109 through 111 for teachers to reproduce or modify. This evaluation can be done at any time during the program, but should be done at a point close to the end. Reading the evaluations is very helpful for teachers, because very often the feedback garnered will help in future planning. Teachers will find that parents/guardians and students alike respond enthusiastically to this new and innovative program. Once teachers have implemented the literature circles program, it will be difficult to imagine ever teaching in a traditional classroom again.

Student and Parent/Guardian
Evaluation of Literature Circles

1. From what your child explained, what do you think about this approach to literature? What do you see as benefits? Drawbacks?

   _____
   _____
   _____
   _____
   _____
   _____

2. Students, what have you learned from literature circles? How have you changed the way you read and the way you respond to reading?

   _____
   _____
   _____
   _____
   _____

3. Students and parents/guardians, compare the journal responses from the beginning with those from the end. Are there any developments in critical thinking about literature? Has the student reached a higher level of comprehension? Give some examples.

Parent/Guardian comments:

   _____
   _____
   _____
   _____
   _____

Student comments:

   _____
   _____
   _____
   _____
   _____

5. Students, as you continue reading in the future, are there any new things that you will be looking for or thinking about as you read? If so, what?

_____

_____

_____

_____

6. Students, read through all your journal entries for your novel. Give yourself a grade for each of the rubric areas, and explain why you earned the grade you did using terminology from the rubric.

Literary Elements Score: _____

Reasons for score: _____

_____

_____

_____

Theme Score: _____

Reasons for score: _____

_____

_____

_____

Interpretation Score: _____

Reasons for score: _____

_____

_____

_____

Making Connections Score: _____

Reasons for score: _____

_____

_____

_____

7. What is your overall evaluation of literature circles? What are the major benefits of doing literature circles as opposed to doing whole class reading and discussion?

Parent/Guardian comments:

_____

_____

_____

_____

_____

_____

Student comments:

_____

_____

_____

_____

_____

_____

Thank you for your time and consideration in completing this survey.

Bibliography

Alverman, D. and Hayes, D. (1989). "Classroom Discussion of Content Area Reading Assignments: An Intervention Study." *Reading Research Quarterly* 24:305–335.

California Department of Education (2001). *Taking Center Stage: A Commitment to Standards-based Education for California's Middle Grades Students.* Sacramento, CA: California Department of Education.

Daniels, H. (1994). *Literature Circles: Voice and Choice in the Student-centered Classroom.* York, ME: Stenhouse Publishers.

Gregory, G.H. & Chapman, C. (2002). *Differentiated Instructional Strategies: One Size Does Not Fit All.* Thousand Oaks, CA: Corwin Press, Inc.

Kendall, J.S., & Marzano, R.J. (2003). *Content Knowledge: A Compendium of Standards and Benchmarks for K–12 Education (4th ed.).* Aurora, CO: Mid-continent Research for Education and Learning. http://www.mcrel.org/standards-benchmarks/.

National Council of Teachers of English and International Reading Association (1996). *Standards for the English Language Arts.* Urbana, IL and Newark, DE: NCTE and IRA.

Peterson, R. & Eeds, M. (1990). *Grand Conversations: Literature Groups in Action.* New York: Scholastic.

Tomlinson, C.A. (1999). *The Differentiated Classroom: Responding to the Needs of All Learners.* Alexandria, VA: Association for Supervision and Curriculum Development.

Tsujimoto, J.I. (1993). "Talk for the Mind." *English Journal* 82:34–37.

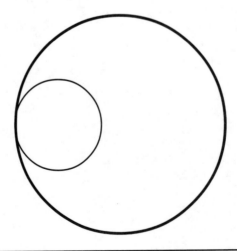